What others have to say about...

The sword of suffering

"As a fellow survivor of cancer, I found that Dr. Stephen Olford has crafted a marvelous text that gives an understanding of God's sovereign grace in the midst of trying circumstances. *The Sword of Suffering* pierces the stigma attached with cancer and suffering and shows how it can be redeemed for the kingdom of God."

DR. E. K. BAILEY
SENIOR MINISTER, CONCORD BAPTIST CHURCH
FOUNDER, E. K. BAILEY MINISTRIES
DALLAS, TEXAS

"Dr. Stephen Olford has helped many of us preachers by modeling what a preacher is—but not all people preach! Now he has ministered to us again by modeling what a sufferer is—and we all suffer! *The Sword of Suffering* is a must for everyone. I could not put it down. It helped me. It encouraged me. It strengthened me."

DR. ROBERT BURCH
SENIOR MINISTER, CALVARY BAPTIST CHURCH
KNOXVILLE, TENNESSEE

"Here is a book on the inevitable hour of suffering we all will face one day, written by a man who has survived the ordeal victoriously. He has a keen insight and a hopeful word for all who suffer. Having gone through a similar crisis myself, I assure you that Stephen Olford knows the trail to find God's answer. To all who suffer, to all who would comfort those who do, this book is *most helpful.* I recommend it wholeheartedly."

DR. LEWIS A. DRUMMOND
BILLY GRAHAM PROFESSOR OF EVANGELISM AND CHURCH GROWTH
BEESON DIVINITY SCHOOL
BIRMINGHAM, ALABAMA

"From the depths of his own personal experience, my longtime friend Stephen Olford has written *The Sword of Suffering* for anyone looking for solace from the pain and anxiety of suffering."

BILLY GRAHAM

"Stephen Olford has given the common denominator of suffering a very powerful numerator—himself. For those sitting in the darkness of emotional, spiritual, physical, and mental pain, *The Sword of Suffering* will help turn on the Light."

MRS. ANNE GRAHAM LOTZ
FOUNDER, ANGEL MINISTRIES
RALEIGH, NORTH CAROLINA

"Pure gold is refined by fire, and this book is pure gold. Stephen Olford has given an incredible and needful gift to the body of Christ. This treasure produced in the furnace of affliction is both profound and practical. Without reservation, I commend this volume to the people of God. The reader will be greatly enriched and will have a desire to share its message with others."

DR. ADRIAN ROGERS
SENIOR MINISTER, BELLEVUE BAPTIST CHURCH
MEMPHIS, TENNESSEE

STEPHEN F. OLFORD

the sword of suffering

ENDURING WORDS OF HOPE, INSPIRATION,
AND HEALING IN THE MIDST OF DESPAIR

AMG *Publishers*

Chattanooga, TN 37422

ISBN 0-89957-845-4 Softcover Edition
ISBN 0-89957-844-6 Hardcover Edition

Library of Congress Control Number: 2001086990

Poem on page 75 from *Toward Jerusalem* by Amy Carmichael. ©1989.
Used by permission of Christian Literature Crusade, Ft. Washington, PA.

Poem on page 111 taken from *Amy Carmichael of Dohnavur* by Frank
Houghton, © 1953 Dohnavur Fellowship (Ft. Washington, PA.: Christian Literature Crusade; London: SPCK). Used by permission.

Cover Design: Phillip Rodgers
Page Design and Layout: Phillip Rodgers and Rick Steele

Printed in the United States of America
06 05 04 03 02 01 –Q– 6 5 4 3 2

This book is dedicated to the glory of God, and with heartfelt

gratitude to "Beloved Physicians". . .

Mark A. Castellaw, MD, Internal Medicine

David W. Dunavant, MD, Surgery

Kirby L. Smith, MD, Oncology

The faithful fellowship of nurses at The Memphis Cancer Center

STEPHEN F. OLFORD

Stephen F. Olford is Founder of **Olford Ministries International** and Senior Lecturer of the **Stephen Olford Center for Biblical Preaching** in Memphis, Tennessee. He is known for his expository preaching and pastoral leadership.

Dr. Olford served as minister of Duke Street Baptist Church in Richmond, Surrey, England (1953–59) and the famed Calvary Baptist Church in New York City (1959–73). He is the voice of *Encounter,* a weekly thirty-minute radio program heard in the United States, Canada, and overseas.

In 1980 Dr. Olford founded the **Institute for Biblical Preaching** to promote biblical preaching and provide practical training for the Christian ministry. Dr. Olford wants to see expository preaching restored to the pulpit, spiritual revival in the church, mobilized evangelism in the world, and righteousness and social justice in our nation.

Dr. Olford has traveled the world, preaching the Word in crusades, conventions, and centers of learning. He holds a doctorate in theology and has been awarded a number of honorary degrees.

As author of numerous books and booklets, Dr. Olford has also contributed to leading periodicals on both sides of the Atlantic. His most recent books are *Not I but Christ*, *The Way of Holiness*, *Anointed Expository Preaching*, and *A Time for Truth*.

Dr. Olford and his wife, Heather, have two sons, Jonathan and David, both of whom are involved in full-time Christian work.

CONTENTS

FOREWORD ix

ACKNOWLEDGMENTS xii

PREFACE xiii

INTRODUCTION xv

THE BIOGRAPHY OF SUFFERING
1. The Reality in Suffering *1*
2. The Anxiety in Suffering *13*
3. The Equality in Suffering *29*
4. The Mortality in Suffering *45*
5. The Vitality in Suffering *63*

THE THEOLOGY OF SUFFERING
Preamble to Chapters Six through Eight *83*
6. The Suffering of the Savior *87*
7. The Suffering of the Saint *103*
8. The Suffering of the Servant *119*

THE PSYCHOLOGY OF SUFFERING
A Psychological Perspective *133*

POSTSCRIPT 141

SELECTED SCRIPTURES 147

THE MEMPHIS CANCER CENTER OVERVIEW 163

"It has to be dark to see the brilliance of the stars."

I t has been stated that weakness, dependency, and suffering are at the core of those things which are perhaps most
abhorrent to Western and specifically American culture. Yet so
much has been written on this topic that our attraction to hearing it
and understanding it seem almost macabre. Numerous tomes including C. S. Lewis's landmark book, *The Problem of Pain,* Phillip
Yancey's *Where is God When It Hurts?,* and James Dobson's *When
God Doesn't Make Sense,* all draw attention to the fact that suffering,
illness, and dependency, while considered inherently natural phe-
nomena, all leave us floundering, insecure, and even questioning the
very underpinnings of our faith—if we had any to begin with.

As is shared in the first portion of this book, the apostle Paul
states in his second letter to the Corinthians:

Blessed be the God and Father of our Lord Jesus
Christ, the Father of mercies and God of *all comfort;*
who comforts us in all our affliction so that we may be
able to comfort those who are in any affliction with
the comfort with which we ourselves are comforted by
God. For just as the sufferings of Christ are ours in
abundance, so also our comfort is abundant through
Christ. (1:3–5, NASB; emphasis mine)

The Scriptures are clear; suffering is a part of life—perhaps all the more so for Christians.

Not only does suffering come to pass that we might experience the abundance of His comforting, but that we might also pass on that abundance to others as we share in their sufferings. Sitting with someone who is suffering may, at times, feel like something akin to the Old Testament picture of sitting in sackcloth and ashes. One of the intents behind the experience of wearing scratchy, abrasive, burlap was that of raising one's awareness of the discomfort of the sufferer. So sitting with and sharing in the sufferings of another raises one's consciousness, sensitivity, and empathic connection with the sufferer and thereby increases one's capacity to show empathy for suffering the world over. It is to this truth that I believe we as Christians have been called, for there is constant suffering that surrounds us. It never goes away! Therefore, my objective is to simply create consciousness by stating that suffering is "essentially essential," and, in so stating, reveal that there is a tremendous value to the dependency of suffering.

This book was borne out of suffering. It is an intimate disclosure of my father's bout with cancer, his journey through the dark, painful, and lonely valleys of physical and mental suffering, and the spiritual battles and struggles that coexisted throughout that journey. It is a story of hope, of atonement, and of redemption, and it reveals lessons that each of us should acquire as we learn the value of weakness.

—Jonathan M. Olford

ACKNOWLEDGMENTS

My special thanks:

To the host of family and friends who prayed fervently for me during my bout with cancer.

To my son, Jonathan M. Olford, Psy.D., Clinical Director, Link Care Center, Fresno, California, who has written the insightful Foreword to this book as well as a concluding section, "A Psychological Perspective."

To Jennifer Balmer, my efficient projects assistant, who typed and prepared the manuscript for publication; and to Victoria Kuhl, my homiletical secretary, who has spent hours in proofreading and offering valuable suggestions.

To my beloved wife, Heather, sweetheart and sufferer with me every moment of my fiery ordeal.

To my merciful and faithful High Priest who sympathized with my illness and weakness with healing grace and power.

"I THANK MY GOD UPON EVERY REMEMBRANCE OF YOU"
(PHILIPPIANS 1:3)

—Stephen F. Olford

What do you do, or where do you turn when the world around you disintegrates? The psalmist's answer is "God is our refuge and strength, A very present help in trouble. Therefore we will not fear, Even though the earth be removed, And though the mountains be carried into the midst of the sea; Though its waters roar and be troubled, Though the mountains shake with its swelling" (Ps. 46:1–3). And, of course, God is our ultimate refuge. That is the spiritual answer. For me, however, there also was and is a medical answer. Through the good services of my personal physician, Dr. Mark A. Castellaw, I was referred to The Memphis Cancer Center under the care of Dr. Kirby L. Smith. Here was a man of God whose "commitment is to the whole person . . . to treat the body, calm the mind, and uplift the spirit." I will never be able to repay my debt of gratitude to this man and his team of doctors and nurses. Conquering cancer was our slogan! "Medicine, miracle, and God" were our undergirding *modus operandi.* The whole experience is chronicled in the pages that follow.

It is at this point of crisis that cancer patients need all that The Memphis Cancer Center provides (see The Memphis Cancer Center Overview, pp. 163–165). For this reason I have elected to contribute all the proceeds of this book to The Memphis Cancer Foundation. Those of you who read these pages and recommend *The Sword of Suffering* to their friends will determine the amount of income invested in this ministry of healing.

May God bless its message and mission far and wide for His glory and the comfort of His people.

—Stephen F. Olford

INTRODUCTION

"A sword will pierce through your . . . soul"
(Luke 2:35; see also vv. 25-34).

wo thousand years ago, a devout man of God entered the temple in Jerusalem to dedicate the Christchild in the presence of the parents, Joseph and Mary. After reciting the beautiful psalm we know today as the *Nunc Dimittis,* he turned to Mary and uttered these prophetic words, "Behold, this Child is destined for the fall and rising of many in Israel, and for a sign which will be spoken against (yes, a sword will pierce through your own soul also), that the thoughts of many hearts may be revealed" (Luke 2:34–35). The image here is of a broad sword striking not her throat, or her chest, but her **soul**—which is "the seat of the sentient element in a man, that by which he perceives, reflects, feels, desires."[1]

---

1. W. E. Vine, *Expository Dictionary of Biblical Words* (Nashville: Thomas Nelson Publishers, 1985), 588.

Do you see the picture? A broad sword piercing through to the soul, which is the "seat of the sentient element." This is why the title of this book is *The Sword of Suffering*. What that sword eventually meant to Mary were not only the verbal insults hurled at her Son during His lifetime, and Israel's rejection of Him; but the ultimate pain, horror, and soul-piercing experience of watching the child of her womb brutally nailed to a Roman cross. That was and is THE SWORD OF SUFFERING.

We live in a desensitized world. In the last century alone, we witnessed two global wars and unceasing localized conflicts on most continents. We have witnessed the holocaust and the killing fields of genocide. In our own country we have witnessed a culture of violence steadily escalate at every level of our society. The killings in our schools, the road-rage shootings on our streets, and seemingly uninhibited murder in our homes, churches, and synagogues are now daily occurrences. Death has become a football to be kicked around with brazen impunity. I have been in social circles where I have witnessed, with shocking disbelief, intelligent people watching a TV newscast featuring a Columbine-like tragedy, a horrifying air crash, a devastating earthquake, or a scene in Africa where skin-and-bone children were breathing their last breaths—while these socialites engaged in frivolous conversation, or raucous laughter! God, have mercy on us!

The dark scenario of the first chapter of Romans is being played out to the letter. Like the toll of a bell, you can hear those solemn words: "God . . . gave them up" (Rom. 1:24, 26), and "God gave them over" (Rom. 1:28). When God acts judgmentally in a consistent sequence of history, His judgment is usually a portent of a swiftly approaching doomsday.

What has all this insensitivity done to the collective psyche of our generation? The answers are many; but for the purpose of this book, I am concerned with *The Sword of Suffering* as it relates to:

The Sensitivity of Suffering

"If one member suffers, all the members suffer with it; or if one member is honored, all the members rejoice with it" (1 Cor. 12:26). In light of the preceding introductory remarks, it is not difficult to understand how the desensitizing process has insidiously affected our generation. However, a pervading lack of sensitivity gives no excuse to those of us who claim to be informed Christians. As we shall discover in succeeding chapters, the Church is a body where we suffer together. Paul says, "If one member suffers, all the members suffer with it" (1 Cor. 12:26). The fact is that we have been "baptized into one body—whether Jews or Greeks [Gentiles], whether slaves or free—and have all been made to drink into one Spirit" (1 Cor. 12:13). The function of the Holy Spirit is to alert the whole family of God to the presence of suffering in any member of that family. Sometimes He uses verbal communication through those who know the situation and report it. This happens all the time in healthy churches. As soon as suffering is detected, the telephones ring, and faxes and e-mails are circulated, and so on. Sometimes there is a God-given premonition concerning a loved one who is in need. As a pastor, such intuition was a normal experience during my times of prayer or reflection. It was my practice to respond immediately to confirm or cancel the signal.

One night, a very unusual signal was deciphered by my wife, Heather, concerning a beloved friend of ours named Dr. W. E. Sangster of Westminster Central Hall, London, England. Dr. Sangster was the greatest "pulpiteer" I ever had the privilege of hearing. He drew, by far, the largest crowds in London, especially during the end of World War II. We often preached together in crusades—with Heather at the piano. Sangster loved to hear Heather play the great hymns of faith. He was also an authority on preaching and wrote two books (now in one volume) called *The Craft of Sermon Construction* and *The Art of Sermon Illustration*.

On this night, Heather was wakened out of her sleep to tell me that Dr. Sangster had just died! We knew for some time that he had a terminal disease. We talked for a few moments about the great man and the preciousness of our friendship, offered prayers, and then went to sleep again. Next morning, the paper man rang our doorbell and shouted, "Paper!" I opened the door, and lying there sprawled out was not our usual *Herald Tribune*, but the *New York Times*—with Dr. W. E. Sangster's picture on the front page along with a two-column obituary! I took the paper to my wife, who could hardly believe her eyes! We figured out the timeline, and, sure enough, this dear man of God had passed away at the identical hour that Heather was awakened! The event reminded us of 1 Corinthians 12:26—"If one member suffers, all the members suffer with it." Such occurrences do not always happen as dramatically as I have recounted; but even across thousands of miles of land and sea, missionaries have reported similar instances.

As I will be saying later in this book, I am so ashamed to have to be reminded by the media that our Christian brothers and sisters are suffering all over the world in an unprecedented manner. More believers sealed their faith with their blood during the twentieth century than at any other time in history.

What has happened to our sensitivity to suffering? The only explanation I can give is that we have grieved and quenched the Holy Spirit in our personal lives as well as the corporate life of the Church (Eph. 4:30; 1 Thess. 5:19). We have allowed the world to squeeze us into its mold (Rom. 12:2). The Bible tells us that "all that is in the world—the lust of the flesh, the lust of the eyes, and the pride of life; is not of the Father but is of the world" (1 John 2:16). Each of these characteristics of worldliness is self-centered. When self is on the throne of our hearts, the Spirit is dethroned, and sensitivity to the needs of others is neutralized. We need to repent of our sins of worldliness, carelessness, and prayerlessness, and with true brokenness return to our "first love" (Rev. 2:4, 5). Failure to do this will hasten the removal of the lampstand from its place of witness, service, and suffering.

The Mystery of Suffering

"The fellowship of the mystery. . . . at my tribulations [sufferings]" (Eph. 3:9, 13). In the New Testament, the Greek word for "mystery" denotes, not the mysterious (as with the English word), but that which, being outside the range of unassisted natural apprehension, can be known only by divine revelation and is made known in a manner and time appointed only by God to those who are illumined by the Spirit. In the context of Ephesians 3:9, the word "mystery" includes human suffering. So Paul adds, "Therefore I ask that you do not lose heart at my tribulations [sufferings] for you, which is your glory" (Eph. 3:13). There is a mystery in suffering that we shall never be able to explain this side of heaven. Nevertheless, such a mystery does not silence the questions that arise when we are face to face with suffering.

I have found there are three helpful words that embody our defense in confronting the mystery of suffering. They are as follows:

1) The Reality of **Sympathy**. "Rejoice with those who rejoice, and weep with those who weep" (Rom. 12:15). Sympathy

is the act or capacity of entering into or sharing the feelings or intentions of another. As fellow sufferers or caregivers, we can never be of help to those in need without the reality of sympathy. This means sharing the feelings of those who are hurting with a reality that rings true. No one can discern hypocrisy and insincerity like a person in pain. When prompted by the Spirit of God, the reality of sympathy penetrates even further into the soul of the sufferer.

2) The Vitality of **Testimony**. "As in water face reflects face, So a man's heart reveals the man" (Prov. 27:19). This means that as in clear water the face of a gazer is reflected, so man finds in his fellow-man the same feelings, sentiments, and passions, which he has himself. It has been my experience as a pastor and caregiver that a simple testimony shared in the power of the Holy Spirit resonates with human need. Such testimony is even more convincing when I have been able to recount similar experiences in the tumbles and triumphs of life. Very often, this opens a way to introduce the gospel.

3) The Authority of **Theodicy**. "I am appointed for the defense of the gospel" (Phil. 1:17). It is important here to define the word "theodicy." It simply means "the defense of God's goodness and power in view of the existence of evil." Caregivers and pastors have to prepare themselves to respond to

suffering and to the theological questions of those who suffer. We have to be thoughtful and tender in our response to such souls. Quoting proof texts often serves no purpose other than to batter the defenseless sufferer who may not be familiar with the Bible. Of course, a recitation of Scripture may be more appropriate when the sufferer receiving counseling is an informed Christian. However, whoever the person may be, the mystery of suffering must be acknowledged. There are many questions we will never answer here on earth. At the same time, I have found the following helpful when theology is the issue:

The Purpose of God in Suffering

"We know that *all* things work together for *good* to those who love God, to those who are the called according to His *purpose*" (Rom. 8:28 emphasis mine). You will notice that I have highlighted three words from this text: "all," "good," and "purpose." The word *all* includes everything that concerns our lives, even suffering. We may not feel that way in the midst of chemotherapy treatment, but God has it checked off on His list of purposeful things. The *good* is the result of the divine alchemy when God "works together" (the Greek implies a pharmacological term) all the ingredients. You will remember the famous words of the Old Testament stalwart Joseph. In spite of all the troubles and horrors he experienced at the hands of his jealous brothers, he could later affirm, "You meant evil against me; but God meant it for good" (Gen. 50:20). Only God can turn the cross into a throne! The *purpose* is clear from the context. We are instructed that "whom He [God] foreknew, He also predestined to be conformed to the image of His Son" (Rom. 8:29). That is the bottom line in God's enfolding drama of redemption. God's business here on earth is to populate heaven with men and women who are like His Son! Suffering is tough, but we must remember that God came to earth in the person of His Son to bring many people to glory and to accomplish this "through sufferings" (Heb. 2:10). We suffer, but Christ suffered for us all!

The Presence of God in Suffering

"In all their affliction He was afflicted, and the Angel of His Presence saved them" (Is. 63:9). When God's ancient people suffered under cruel bondage, God was mindful of them (Ex. 2:25–27); and again, at the time of the judges, God shared the hurt of His redeemed ones (Judg. 10:16). God is always present when people suffer. Think of those brave servants of God—Shadrach, Meshach and Abed-Nego—in the fiery furnace, and then recall the question of Nebuchadnezzar the king, "'Did we not cast three men bound into the midst of the fire? . . . Look! . . . I see *four* men loose, walking in the midst of the fire; and they are not hurt, and the form of the fourth is like the Son of God'" (Dan. 3:19–25; emphasis mine). "The Angel of His Presence" is none other than the Jesus of today!

The Power of God in Suffering

"The Lord stood with me and strengthened me, so that the message might be preached fully through me" (2 Tim. 4:17). These brave words were Paul's testimony at an hour of critical need. In spite of the failure of his friends, Paul was supported by the Lord. Earlier, when God denied the apostle deliverance from "the thorn in the flesh" (the messenger of Satan to buffet him [2 Cor. 12:7]), his faith did not fail because he knew that he would never be forsaken. In his weakness God answered in power so that the apostle could exclaim, "I take pleasure in infirmities. . . . For when I am weak, then I am strong" (2 Cor. 12:10). Paul "heard" a voice saying to him, "My grace is sufficient for you, for My strength is made perfect in weakness" (2 Cor. 12:9).

I can add my own testimony to the foregoing. Yes, in spite of all the doubts, fears, and pain that accompany suffering, God is there in His purpose, His presence, and His power.

This is what this book is all about. We shall examine *The Sword of Suffering* in terms of biography, theology, and psychology.

part one

The Biography of Suffering

CHAPTER ONE

The Reality in Suffering

". . . take the prophets, who spoke in the name of the Lord, as an example of suffering and patience. Indeed we count them blessed who endure" (James 5:10, 11).

These are truly remarkable words. James is calling attention not only to the reality in suffering—it is an example; a fact of life—but James is also calling attention to the reward of suffering, "We count them blessed who endure"!

As one would expect, I have found this to be true, especially with my recent bout with cancer. We already have illustrated how some people literally deny the reality of suffering. The Scriptures, however, repudiate such a notion, and, of course, life is a theater of suffering.

I myself have experienced suffering long before this chapter was written. In my boyhood days in Africa, I was nursed back to life after being stung by one of the most venomous varieties of scorpions. My condition was "touch and go," as I suffered excruciating pain. At least five times, I had serious doses of malaria fever and no access to the drugs we have today. Once I almost died of blackwater fever. Perhaps I was closest to death when a leopard trapped me in my own bedroom! My parents were at a prayer meeting a significant distance away. I was trying to sleep on a very steamy, humid evening. I could stand it no longer, so I went to the window opposite my bed and threw it open. Before I could settle in my bed, a leopard leaped through the open window and eyed me down with full intentions to devour me! Those were not the days of telephones or e-mail, especially in the heart of Africa; but I could pray, albeit only with my eyes open and focused! I could not move nor scream. I know how these cats go for the jugular; they first choke their victims and then they crush

> *"The anxiety of suffering is an apprehension that taxes mind, heart, will and body to the uttermost limit of endurance."*

them. I just tried to stare down the cat. Then something happened. There was a scuffle outside the window and a familiar bark. Our favorite dog had left her pups to come to my aid. That was good; but one of her pups had failed to obey her orders and had followed its mother, and, worse still, jumped through the window into the jaws of the leopard. The pup saved my life! But I suffered tremendous agony.

Agony will be the subject of our next chapter, "The Anxiety in Suffering." It is hard to explain; but I can tell you that such agony is an apprehension that taxes mind, heart, will and body to the uttermost limit of endurance. The anxiety of suffering is a **real** experience.

Now back to my cancer experience. It was about 11:30 AM in my doctor's office in Memphis, Tennessee. Present were Heather, my wife; David, our younger son; and a man I affectionately call "my beloved physician." Dr. Kirby Smith is a famous oncologist who founded The Memphis Cancer Center. I sought his help because a lump under my left arm had revealed through a biopsy and pathology something serious. With genuine professionalism, gracious understanding, and direct candor, my physician looked me straight in the eye and said, "Dr. Olford, you have lymphoma, non-Hodgkin's and aggressively active." Then he added, "Treatment must begin immediately." You could have heard a pin drop in that office after Dr. Smith revealed my diagnosis! Thank goodness, my dear wife broke the tension with a practical remark:

"We have not eaten since early this morning. Do you think we could slip out for a quick lunch?"

"Yes," said the Doctor, with a smile, "but hurry back."

The lunchtime was not a celebration; but it did give us time to pray and hand the whole situation into the hands of a loving, sovereign Lord who knows everything and can do anything He desires.

We hurried back and the doctor himself accompanied us to the treatment lounge with its reclining chairs and stands for IV infusions. As we went through to the lounge, the Doctor cheered my spirit by remarking, "I will now introduce you to my nurses." I have never, and I mean never, met such a **fellowship** of nurses so committed to Jesus and suffering patients. Talk about being positive, prayerful, and patient servants of the Lord! I know them all by name, and can phone those on duty 24 hours day or night.

Soon, I had my first experience of a chemotherapy injection. After three to four hours, I was "unhooked," band-aided and released! As we entered the elevator, I said to Heather, "It wasn't so bad." However, this was just the beginning! Those powerful killing agents had not yet kicked in! Anyone who has not personally experienced chemotherapy treatments has no clue as to what these cycles involve. Four words sum it up for me. They are "fire," "force," "fear," and "faith."

□ **Fire.** When God pronounces judgement on Assyria, Isaiah the prophet uses this line: "The indignation of His anger And *the flame of a devouring fire*"! Only by this means would Assyria be "beaten down" (Is. 30:30, 31). Borrowing this metaphor, I can testify to the fire of chemotherapy. This particular "flame of devouring fire" removed my hair, covered me with burning sores, destroyed my taste buds, almost closed my throat, ulcerated my stomach, and penetrated every part of my body. The dehydration was almost intolerable.

- ❏ **Force.** Conflicts between good and evil and between competing chemical reactions in the body is something that is difficult to describe, but powerful to experience. The battle between good and evil was fought out in Job's incredible battle with suffering. No one can read that book and have any doubt about that. "The LORD said to Satan, 'Have you considered My servant Job?'"—and then added, "stretch out Your hand and touch all that he has" (Job 1:8,11). And we know that Job lost everything but his life. It was the same battle with the apostle Paul when he "pleaded with the Lord three times" for deliverance from the "thorn [stake] in the flesh." Indeed, the New Testament makes it clear that God permitted "a messenger of Satan" to afflict him (see 2 Cor. 12:4–9). Christ's conflict with Satan was evident in His battle on the cross. How could He disarm principalities and powers and make a public spectacle of triumphing over them (Col. 2:15) if there were not a cosmic and titanic battle that took place? The idea that satanic forces often afflict believers is not fiction, but fact. Moreover, the unseen powers that take advantage of God's people in times of suffering are something to be reckoned with. I have experienced those forces surging within my very being.

☐ **Fear.** Yes, fear. The same fear that Job had, Paul had, Jesus had (see Heb. 5:7–9). His godly fear was not only reverent submission for His Father; it was also the normal reaction of His perfect humanity. Yes, it is possible to fear, as we shall see in our next chapter.

☐ **Faith.** This is where all suffering brings us—if we keep our eyes on Jesus. Hebrews 12:1, 2 reminds us that when we look unto Jesus, He becomes the "author and finisher of our faith." Thank God I never wavered in my faith. The song in my heart was "Alleluia! For the Lord God Omnipotent reigns!" (Rev. 19:6).

Here I have to add that I suffered no pain that did not make its mark on my wife, Heather. She is my sweetheart, my wife and homemaker, and brilliant pianist—but not a nurse! And yet she saw me through every visit to the cancer center, as well as fighting sleepless nights with me. On top of all this, she had her hand on every aspect of our ongoing ministry at the Stephen Olford Center for Biblical Preaching here in Memphis, Tennessee—in loyal compliance with our engagement pact to be workers "together with God" (1 Cor. 3:9). Her sweetness, patience, prayers, loyalty, and walk with God—plus her unfailing love—simply beg description.

Throughout this whole ordeal, I have seldom known such precious hours of uninterrupted prayer, worship, and the fruitful study of God's Word. I have written extensively and kept "on top" of my correspondence and every major decision regarding our ministry. "To God be the glory!"

As soon as the diagnosis was made, I wrote to my Board of Trustees and close friends the following letter:

My dear friends,

Grace, mercy, and peace from God the Father and the Lord Jesus Christ, our Savior.

I am taking this first opportunity to share some unpleasant news. I have been diagnosed with lymphoma. The good news is that the disease is . . .

1. Isolated – ALL TESTS show no spread.
2. Incipient – It is at an early stage.
3. Innocuous – It is curable. Praise the Lord!

This development has come as a great shock to Heather, the family and our staff. A swelling under my left arm was the first and only indication of a problem.

Under the sovereign hand of God and in the care of an eminent oncologist, who is a man of God, I am compelled to cancel all commitments that would take me away from the excellent cancer clinic here in Memphis.

As my "extended family" I ask for your prayerful undergirding and personal understanding during the days (and possibly months) that lie ahead. For reasons that I need not extrapolate, I would like you to keep this report within our immediate circle. You know how rumors can grow beyond known facts!

My chief concern is for my sweetheart, Heather, and the family as they seek to cope with this whole situation and its impact upon the ministry.

As for me, the ultimate question is this: What is God allowing, in His permissive will, to make me more like His beloved Son?

Finally, "the Lord God omnipotent REIGNS! Let us be glad and rejoice and give Him glory. . ." (Rev. 19:6, 7).

Heather joins me in assuring you of our warm love and best wishes.

Affectionately,

Stephen F. Olford

One of the replies I received from that letter was from my pastor, Dr. Adrian Rogers, of Bellevue Baptist Church and the *Love Worth Finding* radio broadcast. This is what he said:

Dear Stephen,

You are greatly loved by the Great Physician, as well as your pastor. WE ARE PRAYING, and GOD IS HEALING.

Adrian

Another precious response was from several of my board members who came to my home to anoint me in the name of the Lord and pray for me. I will **never** forget their prayers, the tears, the joys and the power of the Lord that accompanied this healing service. In the midst of the "fellowship of suffering" God gave me the quiet assurance that all was well—but suffering was awaiting me. The "Sword of Suffering" pierced me to the heart. The reality of the matter was that I had *cancer*—but I also had God!

"The reality of the matter was that I had cancer—but I also had God."

Relax in the Arms of God

"The eternal God is your refuge, And underneath are the everlasting arms; He will thrust out the enemy from before you, And will say, 'Destroy!'" (Deut. 33:27).

These words were Moses' ultimate blessing on the twelve tribes, and this is the last of all of them. Here God is depicted as having arms! Think about that for a moment! And the "everlasting arms" are . . .

* **Extensive Arms**—"everlasting arms." They stretch out-wardly to include all His people. No one is left out! Re-flect on this right now. You may feel unwanted or unimportant, but you cannot move out of His reach!

* **Embracive Arms**—"*Underneath* are the everlasting arms." You may feel that you are sinking lower and lower, but you will never sink beyond His embrace—NEVER! Pillow your head in His arms.

✱ **Defensive Arms**—"He will thrust out the enemy from before you." You still may have doubts as to your safety from satanic attacks, but there is no need to fear. God only has to say, "Destroy!"—and you will dwell in safety! All this is from Deuteronomy 33:27, 28. Read these verses over and over again, and remember that His arms are extensive, embracive; yes, and defensive.

RELAX IN THE ARMS OF GOD!

CHAPTER TWO

The Anxiety in Suffering

"Be anxious for nothing, but in everything by prayer and supplication, with thanksgiving, let your requests be made known to God; and the peace of God, which surpasses all understanding, will guard your hearts and minds through Christ Jesus" (Phil. 4:6, 7).

Have you ever been anxious? Before you answer hastily, read again our leading verse at the top of the page!

What appears to be a contradiction between the title of this chapter and our Scripture verses will be resolved before we are through! In the meantime, I am concerned about the insensitivity of the "macho" type, to people who genuinely suffer from anxiety.

Paul was an intense man who, at times, experienced "fear and trembling" (1 Cor. 2:3). I know preachers today who suffer from anxiety. My good friend of more than fifty years, Billy Graham, has invited me many times to travel from one end of the country to the other just to pray for him before he ascended the pulpit, especially at the beginning of a crusade. And I have seen God take over again and again in miraculous ways. Dr. Alan Redpath, former pastor of Moody Memorial Church in Chicago, and now in heaven, shared many a crusade with me in the U.K. and here in the U.S.A. As Dr. Redpath anticipated the responsibility of preaching, he often became visibly sick.

A wonderful couple who had a delightful daughter named Dorothy shared with me the anxiety that almost precipitated a massive heart attack. Dorothy was always on time in coming home at night. Indeed, the father could almost adjust his Rolex watch to her precision timing! One night the ten, eleven, and even twelve midnight bells chimed—yet no Dorothy! Worse still, no phone calls or other warnings. My friend and his wife were *desperate.* The cause of the mix-up is irrelevant at this point; the man almost *died* of panic and anxiety.

When I had quadruple-bypass surgery some years ago, I was anxious the night before. I remember the surgeon coming to my room for a prayer! With my wife Heather and son Jonathan sitting there, he said, "There are three possible options: one, 'a piece of cake'—no problem; two, we could encounter unexpected complications, but we'll deal with these as they emerge; three, see you in heaven!" We chuckled, all right, but I could not wait for the sleeping pill to help alleviate my anxiety.

The same happened before my first chemotherapy treatment. I had to sign a document before the first IV was administered. Now, I implore anyone signing such a document to take a deep breath and read what is before you. Do not skimp!

Chemotherapy Side Effects

<u>Early Side Effects (happens within 24–48 hours)</u>
Flu-like symptoms (fever, chills)
Allergic reactions - itching, redness of skin, chills, shortness of breath
Mild to moderate nausea and vomiting

<u>Late Side Effects (happens within 1–2 weeks)</u>
Dry cough (scarring of the lung)
Hair loss
Mouth sores
Decreased blood counts
Rash
Weakening of heart muscle
Vein discoloration and sclera of eyes (bluish)

The side effects listed above are the most common, but *others may occur.*

With these possible side effects staring you in the face, would you be anxious? I was, and I had to sign the consent form!

Although the Bible is silent about the unconscious mechanisms of anxiety, one thing is clear: Jesus recognized the problem of worry and earthly care. He addressed the issue with these memorable words:

"I say to you, do not worry about your life, what you will eat or what you will drink; nor about your body, what you will put on. Is not life more than food and the body more than clothing? Look at the birds of the air, for they neither sow nor reap nor gather into barns; yet your heavenly Father feeds them. Are you not of more value than they? Which of you by worrying can add one cubit to his stature? So why do you worry about clothing? Consider the lilies of the field, how they grow: they neither toil nor spin; and yet I say to you that even Solomon in all his glory was not arrayed like one of these. Now if God so clothes the grass of the field, which today is, and tomorrow is thrown into the oven, will He not much more clothe you, O you of little faith? Therefore do not worry, saying, 'What shall we eat?' or 'What shall we drink?' or 'What shall we wear?' For after all these things the Gentiles seek. For your heavenly Father knows that you need all these things. But seek first the kingdom of God and His righteousness, and all these things shall be added to you. Therefore do not worry about tomorrow, for tomorrow will worry about its own things. Sufficient for the day is its own trouble." (Matt. 6:25–34)

Commenting on these verses, Dr. A. J. Rainwater III points out that:

> according to the Scriptures, our attention should be fixed upon the ultimate spiritual realities. More than three hundred biblical passages tell us not to fear: Narcissistic self-preoccupation, besides being unnecessary and unrealistic, is a form of self-reliance, and self-reliance is, according to Scripture, sin. The consequences of seeking God's kingdom and righteousness first [are] that our needs are guaranteed to be met (Matt. 6:33). When we seek anything other than God as first priority in our lives, the meeting of our needs is not assured. Seeking Jehovah God first, however, produces the realities of the kingdom of God.[1]

With those weighty words, as a backdrop, let us return to our text and try to resolve what appears to be a contradiction. Paul's words are more than a suggestion; the Greek overtones are: "Stop being anxious for nothing, but in every thing by prayer and supplication, with thanksgiving, let your requests be made known to God; and the peace of God, which surpasses all understanding, will guard your hearts and minds through Christ Jesus" (Phil. 4:6, 7).

---

1. A. J. Rainwater III, *Encyclopedia of Psychology and Counseling,* 2nd ed. (Grand Rapids: Baker Books, 1999), 90.

Quite clearly, we have here the apostle's "shield of faith" to guard against this sword of suffering we call anxiety.

The Problem of Anxiety

"Be anxious for nothing" (Phil. 4:6). Paul is not dodging, but defining the problem. He employs a Greek word that describes the intense pain of mind and body that precedes a violent struggle or contest. In fact, this word, *agon* (from where the English word "agony" derives), was inseparably associated with the ancient Olympic games. Today we talk about the "thrill of victory and the *agony* of defeat." When that agony or anxiety becomes self-preoccupation, it is sin. So Paul has the antidote.

> "When agony or anxiety becomes self-preoccupation, it is sin."

The Prayer of Dependency

"In everything by prayer and supplication, with thanksgiving, let your requests be made known to God" (Phil. 4:6). As Dr. Rainwater so aptly warns, "self-reliance" is the opposite of "prayer reliance" on God. It is amazing how the medical profession is now turning to the therapeutic value of prayer in healing. The prayer of dependency in our text requires three actions on our part, and each one is significant in spelling out true faith dependency:

(1) Tell God about Your Anxiety

"Let your *requests* be made known to God" (Phil. 4:6). I know that the word "requests" has become a "catchall" term for prayer meetings, but the subject of our text is anxiety. There is nothing more comforting and healing than to talk to the Lord about our anxiety. The God who is interested in birds, lilies, and the grass of the field is intensely interested in what is worrying *you* now. Tell Him. As you share, He cares. The very conscious act of transferring your pain, your fears, and your *doubts* to His control is a healing process.

(2) Trust God about Your Anxiety

"Let your requests be made known to God" (Phil. 4:6). Paul is very specific in selecting the verb "known to God." It means, "to certify," "declare," "make known." Trust and confidence are implied in the verb uses. This is the *essence* of dependency. Tell God *everything*—and in telling Him, trust Him, trust for everything.

(3) Thank God about Your Anxiety

"Everything by prayer . . . with thanksgiving" (Phil. 4:6). This is the "bottom line." The sequence goes like this: you thank Him because you trust Him, and you trust Him because you tell Him. If there is a break in this sequence, the whole process is short-circuited. But I say "the bottom line" for another reason. Thanksgiving and praise are healing exercises. There are scores of passages to support this in the Word of God, but one familiar verse delivers quite a punch! Proverbs 17:22 says, "A merry heart does good, like medicine, but a broken spirit dries the bones." The word "medicine" occurs nowhere else in Scripture, but in this context it means "healing," "relief," and "wholeness" and is associated with a cheerful heart. As I pointed out earlier, the medical profession is increasingly coming to see that cheerful and contented dispositions enable a person to resist the attacks of disease and demons. The mind, as we know, has powerful influence over the body. By way of contrast, the second half of the verse reads, "A broken spirit dries the bones." The verb "dries" is used in a variety of ways in the Old Testament. It sometimes refers to vegetation that has lost moisture, or a body that has been drained of energy. The verb is even employed to describe the "dry bones" of Ezekiel 37:11. All this is to remind us that "a merry heart does good, like medicine!" So whatever the circumstances, "in everything [we are to] give thanks; for this is the will of God in Christ Jesus" (1 Thess. 5:18). You will notice that this is not a suggestion; it is an imperative command (see Phil. 4:4)! Obedience to this command, by the enabling of the Holy Spirit, helps to jerk us out of morbidity and pessimism. This brings us to the rest of our text:

The Peace of Tranquility

"The peace of God, which surpasses all understanding, will guard your hearts and minds through Christ Jesus" (Phil. 4:7). The whole world longs for this, but it is the privileged portion of God's dear children and especially those who are suffering anxiety and, therefore, targets of the evil one, who will actually experience this peace.

Let us unpackage these precious words for a moment. The dominant theme is, of course, *the peace of God*. And what about the peace of God? Three things are said or implied:

(1) It Is a Given Peace

"The peace of God" (Phil. 4:7). If you study your Bible carefully, you will find that our relationship to God is both judicial and personal. **Judicially,** we have "peace *with* God" (Rom. 5:1). This is an external, objective reality when God, in grace, on the merits of Christ alone, declares us righteous, justified—once and for all! **Personally,** we can know "the peace *of* God" when we fulfill the conditions that we have been considering as we have worked our way through this text. But it is clear that "the peace of God" can not be manipulated; it is the gift of God.

(2) It Is a Golden Peace

It "surpasses all understanding" (Phil. 4:7). No human words can describe the tranquility, harmony, and restfulness that sweep across the soul when Christ Jesus is enthroned in our hearts and minds. That is why this peace is golden!

(3) It Is a Guarded Peace

"The peace of God . . . will guard your hearts and minds" (Phil. 4:7). Paul's choice of a military term implies that the mind is a battle zone that requires a military unit of soldiers to protect it. Since the purpose of a guard is to prevent outside intrusion or inside confusion, we must count on Christ Jesus, the anointed Savior and Sovereign, to keep us in the "peace of God" day by day; yes, and moment by moment.

There are two illustrative incidents in the New Testament that help us to understand what we mean by the peace of tranquility. Read Mark 4:35–41. After an extremely busy day, the Master, with His disciples, took a boat to cross the Sea of Galilee. "A great windstorm arose, and the waves beat into the boat, so that it was already filling" (v. 37). While all this was going on, Jesus was "in the stern, *asleep on a pillow*" (v. 38). He was in such a deep sleep that the disciples had to literally "shake" (active voice) Him to awaken Him. We know the rest of the story. Jesus arose and rebuked the wind and said to the sea, "Peace, be still!" (v. 39). As far as the disciples were concerned, drowning was inevitable! But Jesus knew how and when He was going to die on the cross for our salvation. *Nothing* was ever going to change that. Therefore, in spite of the storm and rising water in the boat, He was at rest in the will of the Father—"asleep on a pillow." The peace of tranquility guarded His mind and heart. We likewise can know the peace of tranquility when we know that we are in the will of God.

The second incident covers two passages of Scripture (John 21:15–22 and Acts 12:5–19). You will recall that after Peter was restored to fellowship with his Lord—after denying Him with "oaths and curses," Jesus tested him with a threefold challenge to match Peter's threefold denial. Then the Master brought climax to His challenge with this prophetic word: "Most assuredly, I say to you, when you were younger, you girded yourself and walked where you wished; but when you are old, you will stretch out your hands, and another will gird you and carry you where you do not wish." Then the author of this gospel adds, Jesus "spoke [these words], signifying by what death he would glorify God" (John 21:18, 19).

Now let's fast-forward to Acts 12:15–19. Peter has now been restored and revitalized by his Pentecost experience. He has become

God's front man in the building and establishing of the church of Christ, amidst fearful opposition. And, in the sequence of events, we find him in prison awaiting Herod's sword. Because of his VIP status Peter was sleeping, chained to two soldiers; and guards before the door (Acts. 12:6). How could a person, bleeding, chained, and guarded **sleep** with such a "peace of tranquility" so that it had to take the angel of the Lord to strike him in order to awaken him and deliver him from prison? Think back for a moment. Had not the Lord already assured him of the manner in which he would die? With this confidence in his Lord, he could sleep like a "little baby" in circumstances calculated to keep the stoutest spirit awake! Of him it could be written, "And the peace of God, which surpasses all understanding, will guard your hearts and minds through Christ Jesus" (Phil. 4:7).

> *"Of Peter it could be written, 'And the peace of God, which passes all understanding, will guard your hearts and minds through Christ Jesus.'"*
> —Philippians 4:7

Therefore, we have in our text God's antidote to anxiety; and it is not some specious placebo, but rather, "the **peace of God,** which surpasses all understanding." To God be the glory!

Reflect on the Peace of God

"You will keep him in perfect peace, whose mind is stayed on You, because he trusts in You. Trust in the LORD forever, for in YAH, the Lord is everlasting strength" (Is. 26:3, 4).

This is probably one of the best known verses on peace in the prophecy of Isaiah. I look forward to the day when God's ancient people will no longer be daunted with the cities of confusion (Is. 20:5; 24:10; 25:2) but will enter the open gates of a future Jerusalem where only righteous people will enter to worship and rejoice in Jehovah and know "perfect peace."

For believers, this is the city of "perfect peace"; a peace that we can enjoy now through the merits and ministry of our Lord Jesus Christ. So reflect on the peace of God.

* **The Supremacy of This Peace of God**—"[God] will keep him [that's you] in *perfect peace*" (Is. 26:3; italics mine).

Literally the Hebrew (*shalom*) reads, "peace peace." *Shalom* is a very important term in the Old Testament. It is more than a greeting. It occurs more than 234 times and conveys the idea of "completeness," "welfare," and "health." It also signifies a peaceful and prosperous relationship between persons. In your case, it is between God and you. Because of Jesus, you can know "peace with God" (Rom. 5:1) and the "peace of God" (Phil. 4:7). This is why it is called "the perfect peace." Ultimately this peace is more than a state of mind, a philosophy of life, or even a biblical doctrine. This "perfect peace" is *Jesus*, the "Prince of Peace" (Is. 9:6), who wants to reign in your heart and mind, **right now.** Where He reigns there is peace, perfect peace.

✱ **The Sufficiency of This Peace of God**—"[God] will keep [you] in perfect peace, [when your] mind is stayed on [Him]" (Is. 26:3). There are two key words in this part of the verse that are very important to understand. The first is the word "mind." It is not the usual word for our reasoning faculty. It is the word *imagination*. This is highly significant. You know as well as I do that once we are taken captive by our imaginations there is no knowing where we will end up! The devil knows this as well (see 2 Cor. 10:4, 5). This is why our imaginations should be "stayed" on Jehovah! The verb is an unusual one and means "to lean on," "rest on," or "stay on." You will prove the sufficiency of God's peace *only* if you make Jesus, the "Prince of Peace," the object of your repose and rest. As the old hymn puts it:

Stayed upon Jehovah,
Hearts are fully blest:
Finding, as He promised,
Perfect peace and rest.

—Frances Ridley Havergal

✳ **The Security of the Peace of God**—"Trust in the Lord forever, for in YAH, the Lord is everlasting strength [or the Rock of Ages]" (Is. 26:4). Here are some precious thoughts for you. When the prophet Isaiah exhorts you to *trust* in the Lord forever, he uses the name YAH, which is an emphatic designation of God. There is no way to describe His utter trustworthiness and dependability; and it is stated here with emphasis. If that is not enough, the prophet goes on to say, "Trust in the Lord forever . . . the Lord is everlasting strength." The Hebrew word for "strength" means "Rock of Ages." Just as the cleft in the rock provides protection, peace, and provision for the little dove, so our Lord the "Rock of Ages" assures us of the security of the peace of God. These verses (Is. 26:3, 4) inspired Augustus Toplady to compose the well-known hymn, *Rock of Ages*:

Rock of Ages, cleft for me,
Let me hide myself in Thee;
Let the water and the blood,
From Thy riven side which flowed,
Be of sin the double cure,
Cleanse me from its guilt and power.

The wind may blow, the waves may break, the lightening may flash, and the thunder may roar, but you are safe and secure in the cleft of the Rock of Ages. This is "perfect peace!"

REFLECT ON THE PEACE OF GOD.

CHAPTER THREE

The Equality in Suffering

"If one member suffers, all the members suffer with it; or if one member is honored, all the members rejoice with it" (1 Cor. 12:26).

While it is true that God "has made from one blood every nation of men to dwell on all the face of the earth" (Acts 17:26), the words of the apostle in this chapter represent a much more closely-knit fellowship.

Paul learned this very early in his Christian experience. As an archenemy of Jesus and His movement, Saul of Tarsus (as he was called), armed with official papers to drag men and women to prison, was on his way to fulfill his threats when God intervened and transformed his life—and Saul of Tarsus became Paul the apostle. As he was traveling down the Damascus road, "suddenly a light shone around him from heaven. Then he fell to the ground, and heard a voice saying to him, 'Saul, Saul, why are you persecuting Me?'" And his response was, "Who are You, Lord?" Back came the answer, "I am Jesus, whom you are persecuting. It is hard for you to kick against the goads" (Acts 9:3–5). This led to that famous act of submission, "Lord, what do You want me to do?" (Acts 9:6). No one can call Jesus Lord in sincerity and truth without experiencing the transforming miracle of the New Birth (see 1 Cor. 12:3)! In that moment of time, Saul became Paul; the persecutor became the preacher; and the antagonist became the ambassador for Christ. My point in recalling this remarkable record is to dwell on Paul's conversion and his responsive words I just quoted. When Paul, blinded by the heavenly light and kneeling in the dirt of the Damascus highway cried out, "Who are You, Lord?"—a voice from heaven replied, "I am Jesus, whom you are persecuting." In a sense, Paul learned the doctrine of the church in one flash moment! Of course, he had to unpack the full meaning of the doctrine later; but here was Jesus identifying Himself with His suffering followers on earth. "I am Jesus, whom you are persecuting. I am Jesus the *Head* feeling the blows being administered to my *body* on earth!" No wonder Paul could write later, "If one member suffers, all the members suffer with it; or if one

> *"No wonder Paul could later write, 'If one member suffers, all the members suffer with it; or if one member is honored, all the members rejoice with it.'"*

member is honored, all the members rejoice with it" (1 Cor. 12:26); and again, "Rejoice with those who rejoice, *and weep with those who weep*" (Rom. 12:15 emphasis mine).

Later, he could write the theology behind this phenomenon when he declared:

> For as the body is one and has many members, but all the members of that one body, being many, are one body, so also is Christ. For by one Spirit we were all baptized into one body—whether Jews or Greeks, whether slaves or free—and have all been made to drink into one Spirit. For in fact the body is not one member but many. (1 Cor. 12:12–14)

Paul then illustrates this by explaining the equality of *fellowship* and *function*. "If the foot should say, 'Because I am not a hand, I am not of the body,' is it therefore not of the body? And if the ear should say, 'Because I am not an eye, I am not of the body,' is it therefore not of the body?" (1 Cor. 12:15–16). Paul goes on to add other members of the body—but he has made his point. In fellowship and function there is an equality that is both precious to recognize, but powerful to mobilize. We are calling it **equality in suffering**. Observe very carefully how specific Paul is. He states, "If *one* member suffers, *all* the members suffer with it" (1 Cor. 12:26 emphasis added). Pause a moment, and take this in: **one** suffers, **all** suffer with it. Is that quality of life working in your church? Remember, the *global* church includes the *local* church! Do we really identify in suffering with the persecuted church today? Is it not odd, perhaps even unpardonable, that we have had to appeal to Congress and even to the President to intervene on behalf of our tormented and tortured

> "Do we really identify in suffering with the persecuted church today?"

brethren and sisters around the world? Are we victims of a materialistic and desensitized society? Remember our **Head**—even the risen and reigning Lord feels the pain. Can we say that we are partakers of His suffering? As we shall be seeing in a future chapter, Paul's highest ambition was to know Christ and "the fellowship of His sufferings" (Phil. 3:10). Is that your ambition?

All this became overwhelmingly stark to me when cancer was diagnosed in my body. After three or four chemotherapy treatments in the Cancer Center, a new but real world of suffering opened up to me. The "sword of suffering" truly entered my soul and revealed what this chapter is all about—the equalizing power of suffering.

Equality in Suffering Harmonizes Human Division

"God composed the body . . . that there should be no *schism* in the body, but that the members should have the *same* care for one another" (1 Cor. 12:24, 25 italics added). Two words need close attention before we proceed. The term *schism* means "rent" or "division" and describes the contrary condition to what God has designed for the local church in "tempering the body together" (1 Cor. 12:24). The other word is the adjective "same" which is emphatic in Greek. No one in the Body should have special care (except those designed as "less honorable" {1 Cor. 12:23}), but everyone deserves the **same** care. Herein, then, is the equalizing power of suffering.

I had not been in the cancer center lounge (where we received our chemotherapy treatments) for more than four or five times when I observed that suffering harmonizes the human patterns that normally divide people.

The Divisions of Race

"[God] has made from one blood every nation of men to dwell on all the face of the earth" (Acts 17:26). Let me tell you, and let me tell you straight—that cancer is colorblind and is no "respecter of persons." We were all there: black, white, brown and all the colors between. We were a fellowship of sufferers; and only two things mattered—getting well again and *taking care of one another.*

The Divisions of Religion

You name them, they were all there: Protestant, Catholic, non-religious and a variety of denominations. But to me the astonishing fact was that it mattered little what religious background or beliefs were represented, we were **all** facing death or life; and, like it or not, **no one** could rule out the **God factor**. Suffering has a way of bringing men and women to the place where all suffering is totaled—the cross of Christ. Hardly a day went by when someone was not led to Christ by the pastor who is part of the staff!

The Divisions of Rank

When God created the body, which is the church of Christ, he made "Jews or Greeks . . . slaves or free . . . to drink into one Spirit" (1 Cor. 12:13). This expression "Jews or Greeks . . . slaves or free" echoes Paul's teaching that men and women whatever status or rank in life, have equal access by grace alone, through faith alone into God's "so great salvation" (Heb. 2:3 KJV). I can tell you if ethnicity was neutralized, so was elitism. Most people dressed in casual clothes for their treatments, but it was not difficult to spot the "well-heeled." But, my reader friend, that wealth was not worth a dime as patients absorbed the powerful chemicals calculated to kill the patient if not the cancer! The threshold of suffering is **level**— whomever you are! All this produced in me such emotions and sensitivity to my fellow sufferers that most of the time I was on the verge of tears.

Another aspect of this equalizing power of suffering is that:

Equality of Suffering Mobilizes Devotion

"If one member suffers, all the members suffer with it" (1 Cor. 12:26). Although those words are addressed to a local church, I saw the principle inherent in the words of the apostle dramatically "fleshed out" in a cancer center lounge in Memphis, Tennessee. The passions of devotion were expressed at one point or another from everyone in our "fellowship of sufferers"—and in some cases from the most unexpected sources. Three monosyllabic words help to sum it up:

The Equality of HOPE

"Hope does not disappoint" (Rom. 5:5). When Paul celebrates a hope that can never disappoint, he has reached a climax of character building that is based on the grace of God. He has described the maturing of character—overflowing with the love of God. So in quoting this verse, we are not out of line. The equality of hope in suffering can come only through the testing of character in the fires of suffering and the power of the Holy Spirit. Let me give several examples.

A well-known contractor in town heard I was at the cancer center and came to see me. Several years ago, he did excellent work on my study at the Stephen Olford Center for

Biblical Preaching. I can remember the days when he never appeared without a cap! He had serious cancer. It had spread, and the prognosis was not good. Nevertheless, he was prayed for and submitted to heavy chemotherapy. That was some time ago. Now he was sitting alongside of me as the IV needle delivered its powerful destroying agents to my body. He told me he was now **clean of cancer!** Full of hope, he had come to encourage me and pray for me. In fact, he was leaving for Haiti the next day on a missionary trip. Here was the "equality of hope" creating hope in me!

Several days later, Heather and I were checking in at the reception desk when the wife of a well-known pastor in Memphis greeted us with obvious exuberance. She had just been declared cured and had come in for her regular checkup. She had undergone a mastectomy and some spread of cancer, but was now cancer-free and back to normal living. Here was another "hand of hope" reaching out to me. You cannot imagine what this means to a cancer patient. To many, the very word "cancer" is synonymous with death.

Perhaps the most dramatic example of the equality of hope is the story of a pastor. His testimony will appear in full in chapter five. His contribution to "hope" building is that he is around all the time, cheering the patients and caring for their souls as the need arises. He reached the "hopeless" state himself several times and, therefore, was never expected to live. I am pleased to tell you that he is now the picture of health. You will enjoy his story.

The Equality of HURT

"If one member suffers, all the members suffer with it" (1 Cor. 12:26). I cannot think of a more agonizing spectacle than to watch, for hours, sufferers who do not appear to be improving. I have no shame in confessing that I witnessed such suffering with tears trickling down my face. Here hope turns into **hurt**.

The ultimate example of "hurt" arose when the doctor with grave face came out from the curtained hospital bed and hurried to his office. Presently from that bed a feeble voice cried, "Is there no hope?" Instantly, the pastor who was talking to me hastened to the woman's bedside and with comforting words quietly led this dear soul to the joy, peace, and certainty of faith in Jesus Christ! She was now headed to perfect and permanent healing, to a place where there was no more hurt or tears.

The Equality of HELP

"As we have opportunity, let us do good to all, especially to those who are of the household of faith" (Gal. 6:10). If there is a force under God that mobilizes devotion and action, it is the force of suffering. Think of the calamities and catastrophes that have taken place in recent years in countries both near and far. The national and international responses to help and heal have been nothing less than phenomenal. But I have witnessed such benevolent responses in a cancer clinic. There has been no occasion when I have been present at the clinic, where "the equality of help" principle has not been operative. The care of one patient for the other is beautiful to behold! I will add that such care does not exist between good friends only. Strangers or newcomers are treated the same way without hesitancy or discrimination. Acts of kindness abound, whether it be in the form of a drink of coffee or water, a blanket to cover those who feel cold, an offer to help a patient to the restroom—on and on I could go. There is something about suffering that sensitizes the human spirit. Even Jesus wept in the presence of suffering (John 11:35).

I want to fictionalize a scenario I visualized one afternoon during an unusually long chemotherapy treatment. A popular government official made an outrageous statement on national television that Christians were intellectually weak and required the emotional support and strength of one another and their churches. This is a paraphrase of what this man said with arrogant overtones. As I sat there musing, in my reverie, I saw this gentleman diagnosed with an extremely aggressive cancer. His huge body and carriage were already reduced to "humiliating helplessness." He sought top medical help, and of all the places in the U.S.A, he came to the Memphis Cancer Center. During my imaginative processes, I found myself during a treatment session sitting opposite him! I recalled his statement concerning the "weak" intellects of Christians. Then I reflected on the great minds of biblical characters like Abraham, Moses, David, Solomon (the most informed man in all the world), the prophets, the brilliant mind of Paul—then Augustine, Calvin, Luther—theological giants who have defined and directed all civilized thought to this day. I threw in a few more names better known to him—C. S. Lewis, Sir Winston Churchill, and Margaret Thatcher—all three personally known to me. I wondered how a mind could be so distorted and devoid of historical information as to overlook towering personalities such as I listed. Just then, my absorption with the great minds of Christendom was interrupted. I looked up and could hear him saying in a whisper, "Water . . . water." Although harnessed to my IV hookup, I fetched him water, which he consumed with a gulp. Later he asked for a blanket; I signaled to one of the fine Christian nurses, and she did the favor. An hour later, he leaned forward and pointed to the men's room. By this time I was free of my IV hookup. So I helped him to the men's room and back to his recliner. As we were returning, he looked me in the eye and said, "You are kind, and I thank you. Who are you, and what are you doing here?" I quietly replied, "I am fighting cancer like you are; but I have one advantage, I'm a Christian, with all the resources of a strong mind, unspeakable peace, and a sure hope for today and eternity." He hobbled back with my help to his recliner. His last words were: "I'm glad you're a Christian. I've never been in a place like this where everybody is so cheerful and caring! Thank you *so* much." And there were tears in his eyes!

My "reverie" illustrates the fact that the equality of suffering mobilizes a devotion of fellow-feeling for others. As a human being, leave alone a Christian, I could not in all good conscience ignore my fellow sufferer. The text that heads this chapter (1 Cor. 12:26ff.) points out that when suffering comes to one part of the body (physical or spiritual) it affects the well-being of the whole. God has made us this way in order that we might care for one another.

Remember the People of God

"Remember the prisoners *as if chained with them*—those who are mistreated—since you yourselves are in the body also" (Heb. 13:3 emphasis added).

This is one of the moral directives we find in the closing chapter of the epistle to the Hebrews. After exhorting us to practice "brotherly love" and not to forget to entertain strangers (13:1, 2), the writer issues this imperative: "Remember the prisoners *as if chained with them*" (13:3). This has been the theme of this book—the idea of identifying with the "sword of suffering." The prisoners here are believers who are being mistreated and persecuted. And we know that "if one member suffers, all the members suffer with it" (1 Cor. 12:26). One of the best therapeutic exercises for any sufferer is to think of others or to remember others.

★ **Remember Your Enemies.** "Love your enemies" (Matt. 5:44). Yes, we may hate their sins, but we are to love them as *souls* for whom Christ died. This may be a novel way of reaching people for Christ, but I can testify to its effectiveness. Through correctional officials or names referred to you by Christian radio stations, write to these individuals and pray for them. You will be amazed how absorbed you will become and how responsive these so-called "hardened criminals" really are. It is not only possible that you will bring them to a saving faith in Christ, but they will likely develop a hunger for God's Word and sound teaching that you rarely find in your local church.

✳ **Remember Your Neighbors.** "You shall love your neighbor" (Matt. 5:43). Think of the names and addresses—even phone numbers, of your neighbors, and pray for them by name. Recall the way you have overlooked their spiritual needs—although you were so close to them. Target them for Christ. Bring them into your suffering and share your triumphant faith in Christ. Remember this is a vulnerable time in their relationship to you.

✳ **Remember Your Friends.** "Let us do good to all, especially to those who are of the household of faith" (Gal. 6:10). Design a prayer list of your friends and list them alphabetically in a convenient rotation such as the days of a month. Write your friends, ask them for prayer requests, and suggest that they respond with answers to your prayers! This will develop your prayer life and, at the same time, forge bonds of fellowship that will last forever, even after God has called you home.

* **Remember Your Family.** "Praying always with all prayer . . . for all the saints" (Eph. 6:18). In that category of "all saints" you can include your family, which is your first priority in prayer. There may be unsaved members, unfulfilled members, or unconcerned members. Whatever the need and whatever the cost, make them the burden of your intercessions and supplications. If you are suffering with cancer, chemotherapy treatments can take a *lot* of time! Why not invest some of that time, then, to "pray through" for every loved one in your family?

Believe me, these disciplined exercises that I have suggested will not only prove to be physically and personally therapeutic, but spiritually and redemptively dynamic—under the good hand of our God. So very simply, but sincerely I say: *"Remember others."*

REMEMBER THE PEOPLE OF GOD!

CHAPTER FOUR

The Mortality in Suffering

"It is appointed for men to die once, but after this the judgment"
(Heb. 9:27).

Mortality in suffering is an inescapable reality for all of us—unless God intervenes. Enoch and Elijah were spared death (2 Kings 2:11; Heb. 11:5). And, in a limited way, so were people like Lazarus (see also Luke 7:21; 8:55) and the multitudes who were resuscitated at Christ's resurrection (John 11:43, 44; Matt. 27:51–53). Others could be mentioned. The climatic exception will be the rapture of the Church (1 Thess. 4:17), when living saints will be "changed in a moment" and "caught up" to meet the Lord in the air and ever after be with the Lord (1 Cor. 15:51, 52; 1 Thess. 4:17).

> *"Mortality in suffering is an inescapable reality for all of us—unless God intervenes."*

With that brief qualifying overview, we now approach the sensitive subject of death with the understanding that "it is appointed for men to die once" (Heb. 9:27). Within the permissive will of God, life can be lengthened or shortened, but death inevitably follows. Within this equation, are the two factors of illness and wellness. There are those who argue that there should be no sickness for the believer. But the facts of Scripture and history repudiate such a notion. Why would we be exhorted to pray for the sick, if believers are never sick? At this point, I urge you to read James 5:13–16:

> Is anyone among you suffering? Let him pray. Is anyone cheerful? Let him sing psalms. Is anyone among you sick? Let him call for the elders of the church, and let them pray over him, anointing him with oil in the name of the Lord. And the prayer of faith will save the sick, and the Lord will raise him up. And if he has committed sins, he will be forgiven. Confess your trespasses to one another, and pray for one another, that you may be healed. The effective, fervent prayer of a righteous man avails much.

As a pastor and evangelist, I have acted upon these divine instructions on the mission field, pastorates, and even in my crusades and seen God work miraculously in granting healing without medical intervention. I have also witnessed occasions when God, for His own purposes, has withheld His healing touch. In each instance, our heart preparation and exercise of simple faith have been as genuine as we know how. For this reason, I deprecate the claims of some who challenge the faith of sufferers who do not receive healing.

Only God Heals

Sometimes God Heals Directly. "I am the LORD who heals you" (Ex. 15:26). As God transformed the bitterness of the waters of Marah, so He promises to preserve His people from illness (Ex. 23:25). The Jehovah Name of *Kapha* testifies to the mercy and power of God to heal His people—without human intervention. Innumerable times I have witnessed this process of healing in the jungles of Central Africa, when medicines were exhausted or nonexistent. God used the "built-in" resources of the human body to heal all manner of illnesses and wounds. This healing, of course, is effected through the quickening work of the Holy Spirit both now and in that resurrection day to come (Rom. 8:11).

Sometimes God Heals Medicinally. "Keep yourself pure. No longer drink only water, but use a little wine for your stomach's sake and your frequent infirmities" (1 Tim. 5:22, 23). Water in ancient times was often polluted and carried many diseases. Therefore, Paul advised his young colleague to use wine as a disinfectant against the harmful effects of impure water. Paul believed in the value of medical advice and practice. He could refer to Dr. Luke as "the beloved physician" (Col. 4:14). Luke was the apostle's constant companion on his missionary travels. As my oncologist has reminded me many times: whether it's medicine or miracle, God alone heals!

Sometimes God Heals Pastorally. "Is anyone among you sick? Let him call for the elders of the church, and let them pray over him, anointing him with oil in the name of the Lord" (James 5:14; see context also). James was a man of prayer. This is evident by the number of times he refers to the subject of prayer. Indeed, tradition informs us that when James' body was being prepared for burial, his loved ones noticed the heavy calluses on his knees. Since then and throughout the centuries, he has been known as "Camel Knees."

In the instructions given us here for healing services in *the local church,* the emphasis is on "the prayer of faith" (v. 15). Five steps are listed:

There Must Be the Prayer of Affinity.

"Call for the elders of the church" (James 5:14). Remember our last chapter? "If one member suffers, all the members suffer with it" (1 Cor. 12:26). "The elders" represent that sensitivity and affinity. This is not a function where the healing initiative is relegated to some famous healer.

There Must Be the Prayer of Authority.

"Pray . . . in the name of the Lord" (14). We may pray, and we may exercise faith, but only God heals! "The name of the Lord" represents the authority of Father, Son and Holy Spirit for the accomplishment of His redemptive purpose for *His glory alone.*

There Must Be the Prayer of Ability.

"Pray . . . anointing" (v. 14). The word "anointing" here suggests "rubbing" rather than "pouring," but that observation is irrelevant. In the context of fellowship and prayer, the oil most likely refers to the healing power of the Holy Spirit, who alone can "give life to [our] mortal bodies" (Rom. 8:11). Herein, therefore, is the "ability" in prayer. For as Paul reminds us, "The Spirit also helps in our weaknesses. For we do not know what we should pray for as we ought, but the Spirit Himself makes intercession for us with groanings which cannot be uttered" (Rom. 8:26).

There Must Be the Prayer of Accountability.

"Confess your trespasses" (James 5:16). Any sin that blocks the blessing must be confessed on the basis of 1 John 1:9. This applies to the elders, the sufferer and the supporters in prayer. We must remember that if we "regard iniquity in [our] heart, the Lord will not hear" (Ps. 66:18).

There Must Be the Prayer of Assurance.

"The Lord will raise him up" (James 5:15). The reason for this assurance is given us in this very passage. "The effective, fervent prayer of a righteous man avails much" (v. 16). Jesus assured us that "whatever things [we] ask when [we] pray, believe that [we] receive them, and [we] will have them" (Mark 11:24).

After many years in the ministry, those simple instructions have never failed to reveal God's will in the matter of healing. Ultimately, God alone heals. This leads to our last point:

Sometimes God Heals Finally. Paul put it this way, "I am hard pressed between the two, having a desire to depart and be with Christ, which is far better" (Phil. 1:23). The apostle tells us that while it was "good" (or needful) to remain with his fellow saints in Philippi, it was "far better" to be with Christ! In His presence is perfect and **permanent** healing. No more pain, tears, or death. Why is it so many Christians do not see it that way? "Healing" down here is only temporary at the best, and with the healing we have to endure the same struggles, sickness, and suffering.

What is even more important to recognize is that suffering is a gift from God. The Word is clear, "To you it has been granted on behalf of Christ, not only to believe in Him, but also to suffer for His sake" (Phil. 1:29). In His inscrutable wisdom, God has chosen suffering to accomplish His purposes both in His Son (see Heb. 2:10) and in His children (see 1 Pet. 1:6,7). Suffering matures us in the present (James 1:2–4) and glorifies us in the future (Rom. 8:17), as we share with Christ in "the fellowship of His suffering" (Phil. 3:10).

The idea that we can actually benefit from suffering is a far cry from today's "health and wealth gospel." The "name it and claim it" teachers don't quite know what to do with this approach to suffering. The fact that God's "perfect will" has permitted sickness and poverty for the choicest saints throughout history does not seem to register with these teachers! God's will certainly included poverty for Christ, who was born in a stable and had nowhere to lay his head during His lifetime. God's will also included tragedy, culminating in Christ's death on the cross (see Phil. 2:8). Suffering, therefore, is part of "the determined" plan of God (Acts 2:23).

> *"The idea that we can actually benefit from suffering is a far cry from today's 'health and wealth gospel.'"*

This "prosperity gospel" is a cruel message. We should not refer to this teaching as "gospel," for it is not "good news" at all. It wrongly informs people that they are suffering the loss of personal health and wealth because of their lack of faith. Tell that to Job, who lost *everything* and yet could affirm, "Though He slay me, yet will I trust Him" (Job 13:15). Tell that to Moses, who chose to "suffer affliction with the people of God rather than to enjoy the passing pleasures of sin, esteeming the reproach of Christ greater riches than the treasures of Egypt" (Heb. 11:25, 26). Tell that to the host of martyrs who "were stoned, . . . sawn in two, were tempted, were slain with the sword." (Heb. 11:37, 38). Tell that to Paul, who gloried in the "loss of all things" that he might "gain Christ" (Phil. 3:8).

I can remember speaking at a nationwide convention of many thousands. Before the keynote address, a national celebrity was introduced to give her testimony. The young lady had been involved in a life-threatening car accident, and had recovered miraculously. Her story was most moving and Christ-exalting, but one sweeping statement that she made greatly disturbed me. Without any qualification, she looked across the sea of faces and said, "What God has done for me, He can do for you—*if you only have the faith.*" In that moment, I thought of people like Joni Erickson Tada in her wheelchair and scores of other lesser-known personalities. I have to admit that before I could expound God's Word to that waiting audience, I had to set the record straight. God gave grace, words and tone to win people's hearts, including the young lady who testified. Only God heals, and only He can determine how, when and whom.

This chapter would not be complete, however, without touching on the subject of death itself. After all, our theme for this chapter is *mortality in suffering*.

Where better can we go than to the most explicit record of our Savior's encounter with death as chronicled by the apostle John (11:1–44). It would help you enormously if you paused now to read these verses. Here we have:

The Master of Mortality (John 11:1–44)

The raising of Lazarus from the dead in John 11 has been called the capstone of Christ's ministry on earth. Our concern here, however, is the detailed manner in which our Lord coped with death.

Christ Was Master of News in the Presence of Death

"Lord, behold, he whom You love is sick" (v. 3). "Lazarus is dead" (v. 14). Christ received the news factually, but not fatally. How we receive news of the death of a loved one or some important figure on the national or international scene is so important. Even as I write, my younger brother, John, has passed away in his sleep in far-off Wales. My older brother, Paul was so overwhelmed; he was unable to phone, and almost had a heart attack! However, the news came through loud and clear, and I've taken the necessary measures appropriately. It matters how we react. Jesus had a plan. We know

He was and is omniscient, but what followed shows that He had a plan of procedure (see vv. 6, 7). He determined that this tragedy would become a victory. Mark carefully His words, "This sickness is not unto death, but for the glory of God, that the Son of God may be glorified through it" (v. 4). By raising Lazarus from the dead, Jesus would demonstrate His deity in an undeniable way.

Christ Was Master of Doubts in the Presence of Death

"Then Thomas . . . said to his fellow disciples, 'Let us also go, that we may die with Him' " (v. 16). While Thomas's words reflect loyal devotion, they also reveal the doubts and pessimism that were in his heart and, in all probability, in the hearts of the other disciples. As you read the context, you will agree that Thomas's fears were legitimate. Bitter hostility toward Jesus was growing, and the journey to Bethany was not without grave danger (see v. 8). Who has not faced death without "all hell breaking loose"? Not only doubts and fears, but also the complications mixed with sorrow that disrupt the daily routine.

The answer of Jesus to all of this was, "Our friend Lazarus sleeps, but I go that I may wake him up" (v. 11). These words are immediately preceded with the clearest statement concerning the ordered life of Jesus: "Are there not twelve hours in the day? If anyone walks in the day, he does not stumble, because he sees the light of this world. But if one walks in the night, he stumbles, because the light is not in him" (vv. 9, 10). Using a well-known proverb, Jesus employed it to teach three principles in "the ordered life": first, we must **find** God's will, (". . . sees the light of this world" [v. 9]); secondly, we must **follow** God's way, ("walks in the day"[v. 9]); and thirdly, we must **finish** God's work, ("twelve hours in the day" [v. 9]). To do anything less is to go forth into the night and stumble. How can doubts remain in the presence of such an "ordered life"?

Christ Was Master of Grief in the Presence of Death

"Jesus wept" (v. 35). The Greek reads, "Jesus shed tears." He did not weep aloud like the professional mourners. His tears represented compassionate identification with His loved ones Mary and Martha, but, at the same time, produced indignation among His critics. Tears often tell more than talk. In fact, in my many years of pastoral work, words have often failed me; all I could do was weep.

Christ Was Master of Faith in the Presence of Death

Jesus said, "I am the resurrection and the life. He who believes in Me, though he may die, he shall live. And whoever lives and believes in Me shall never die" (vv. 25, 26). This is the fifth of the seven great "I AM" claims of Christ in John's gospel. With this statement, Jesus moved Martha and Mary from an abstract belief in the resurrection to a personalized trust in the Lord of life. Faith is begotten in the human heart when the risen Lord becomes real (Rom. 10:9).

Christ Was Master of Hope in the Presence of Death

"Lazarus, come forth!" (John 11:43). Jesus had already affirmed His claim as Resurrection and Life (v. 25), but now He demonstrates the claim! Jesus cried with a loud voice, "Lazarus, come forth!" Augustine once said that if Jesus had not designated Lazarus by name, all the graves would have been emptied at His command.[1] All this led up to a climactic moment in time, and the miraculous result was a celebration of hope! Again, what a message and spirit to bring to people in the presence of death! We don't need a Lazarus to come forth from a tomb; we have Jesus—alive, available, and adequate right here and now!

We know the rest of the story of the reunion and rejoicing (see John 12:1, 2), but enough has been said to show that Christ is Master of Mortality. He is the same Jesus as the One who stood by the tomb.

---

1. *The Nelson Study Bible: New King James Version*, Earl D. Radmacher, ed., (Nashville: Thomas Nelson Publishers, 1997), 1945.

By His Holy Spirit He can use us to inspire hope to the hopeless—because we do not "sorrow as others who have no hope" (1 Thess. 4:13).

The "sword of suffering" is never more "sharp and two-edged" as when we face death, but thank God we have "a great High Priest" alive and present. He sympathizes with our weakness, because He was tested in all points as we are, though He never sinned. So at any moment, we can come boldly to the throne of grace to obtain mercy and find grace to help in times of need (see Heb. 4:14–16). Hallelujah!

> *"Christ sympathizes with our weaknesses, because He was tested in all points as we are—though He never sinned."*

Relate to the Power of God

"That I may know Him and the power of His resurrection" (Phil. 3:10).

Paul dictated these words at the end of his life. He had written theology, traveled endless miles for the cause of the gospel, languished in prison for his faith, established churches on his missionary journeys—and yet, here, he expresses his highest ambition—to know Christ and the power of His resurrection. What is also important to realize is the fact that Paul anticipated his own death. He writes, "I am hard pressed between the two, having a desire to depart and be with Christ, which is far better" (Phil. 1:23).

In what sense does the power of God help when you are facing sickness, suffering, and separation? Jesus anticipated the answers to that question before He went to Calvary when He promised. . . .

The Power of Comfort in the Spirit. "I will pray the Father, and he shall give you another Comforter" (John 14:16, KJV). The name "Comforter" means, "one called alongside to *help*." Jesus added by way of application, "I will not leave you comfortless; I will come to you" (John 14:18, KJV). What a promise! All that Jesus was and is was included in the gift of the Holy Spirit. The apostle Paul refers to "the power of the Spirit of God" (Rom. 15:19), and he also informs us that it was the Spirit "who raised Jesus from the dead" (Rom. 8:11; see also Eph. 1:19). Put that all together, and you have the power of comfort. Right now, in your loneliness and depression, claim what is yours!—the Spirit of power to comfort you. His very name "Comforter" spells out His ministry to you even as you read the words, "One called alongside to help."

The Power of Caring in the Spirit. "God of all comfort, who comforts us in all our tribulation, that we may be able to comfort those who are in any trouble" (2 Cor. 1:3, 4). We have touched on this subject before, but it is worthy of repetition. No one has the "power to care" like the sufferer. It has been said, "God comforts us not only to make us comfortable, but also to make us comforters."[2] The power of caring can be effective only when empowered by the Holy Spirit. The comfort that God gives to us becomes a gift we can give to others (see 2 Cor. 7:6; Acts 9:10–19). So your willingness to share the power of caring reflects the sincerity of your faith (see John 13:35). In addition to this, it transfers your attention from

---

2. *The Nelson Study Bible: New King James Version*, Earl D. Radmacher, ed., (Nashville: Thomas Nelson Publishers, 1997), 1787.

yourself to others who are blessed by your ministry. As I took my chemotherapy treatment at The Memphis Cancer Center, I saw this "transferred attention" ministry in action—over and over again.

The Power of Conquering in the Spirit. "We are more than conquerors through Him who loved us" (Rom. 8:37). The words are in the context of Christ's redemptive acts—"Christ who died . . . is also risen, who is even at the right hand of God, who also makes intercession for us" (Rom. 8:34). The power of the resurrection assures us of victory over "death . . . life, . . . angels, . . . principalities . . . powers, . . . things present . . . things to come . . . height . . . depth, . . . [and] any other created thing" (Rom. 8:38, 39). Sit back and reflect on these wonderful facts . . .

1) Nothing can separate you from God's love

2) Nothing can change your status as a child of God—predestined, called, justified, and glorified (Rom. 8:30).

3) Nothing can rob you of all that there is in Jesus. "[God] who did not spare His own Son, but delivered Him up for us all, how shall He not with Him also freely give us all things?" (Rom. 8:32).

EVERYTHING is in Jesus—and Jesus is EVERYTHING.

RELATE TO THE POWER OF GOD!

THE SWORD OF SUFFERING

CHAPTER FIVE

The Vitality in Suffering

"For to you it has been granted on behalf of Christ, not only to believe in Him, but also to suffer for His sake" (Phil. 1:29).

O ur key verse shocks most Christians who have not seen it before, or do not understand the significance of The Sword of Suffering. But there it is—suffering is a "gift of grace" which brings vitality into our lives (2 Cor. 7:9, 10; 1 Pet. 5:10), and in a day to come, eternal reward (1 Pet. 4:13). Yes, suffering is part of God's redemptive plan for **all** His children. Some of us try to dodge it, but that only brings tragedy instead of victory.

When I was a teenager on a mission station in Central Africa, I had many wild animal "pets." In fact, I ran a small zoo! One of my special interests was mounting beautiful butterflies. One species was difficult to capture. We called it the "bush-butterfly." It was huge and displayed on its wings the most vivid and attractive colors. Through negotiations with one of my African friends, I secured some cocoons of this particular butterfly that were ready to hatch. One morning I went to examine my cocoons and observed that one of them was indeed hatching. A terrific struggle was going on. In my ignorance, I snipped the cocoon where a small aperture appeared. A little while later, I returned to watch my beautiful butterfly emerge. To my horror, I saw a moist caterpillar wriggle out of the cocoon with helpless wings and no color! I thought I was saving the butterfly from suffering, but suffering was the only way to force the latent fluids in its body to fill those wings and make the butterfly take to the air in all its beauty and glory. One of the definitions of the word "metamorphosis" is "a pronounced change effected by *pressure.*" I had relieved the pressure and killed my butterfly. Instead of the *vitality* of suffering, I had caused the *catastrophe* of suffering.

> "Suffering is part of God's redemptive plan for all His children."

There is a vitality of suffering which is implicit in the theology of suffering. We have seen this as we have examined briefly several aspects that appear in the New Testament, where the common word for suffering occurs forty-two times. As we proceed, let us never forget that the Christian message is in part the unveiling of the suffering God.

STEPHEN F. OLFORD

The apostle Peter writes, "Christ also suffered once for sins, the just for the unjust, that He might bring us to God, being put to death in the flesh but made alive by the Spirit" (1 Pet. 3:18). Out of His suffering comes life; and, to a finite degree, out of our suffering for Him and with Him, we can know life, vitality, and victory.

The Vitality of Suffering through Persecution

> Blessed are you when they revile and persecute
> you, and say all kinds of evil against you falsely for My
> sake. Rejoice and be exceedingly glad, for great is your
> reward in heaven, for so they persecuted the prophets
> who were before you. You are the salt of the earth; but
> if the salt loses its flavor, how shall it be seasoned? It is
> then good for nothing but to be thrown out and tram-
> pled underfoot by men. (Matt. 5:11–13)

Persecution is not something to be sought, but it is something to be expected by those who live godly lives. The Bible says, "All who desire to live godly in Christ Jesus will suffer persecution" (2 Tim. 3:12). The word "persecution" here literally means "hunted" or "pursued"; and, of course, this explains the story of persecuted martyrs through the centuries and especially in our time in countries that oppress the gospel. Nevertheless, as

"All who desire to live godly in Christ Jesus will suffer persecution."
(2 Tim. 3:12)

always, the blood of the martyrs has determined the vitality and good of the Church. In the words of Jesus, there is the growth of "the kingdom" down here and a "great . . . reward in heaven" for "those who are persecuted for righteousness' sake" (Matt. 5:10, 12).

The Vitality of Suffering through Tribulation

"In the world you will have tribulation; but be of good cheer, I [the Lord Jesus] have overcome the world" (John 16:33). Although the word "tribulation" is sometimes used to include persecution, it has an identity of its own. It means "pressure" and figuratively conveys the idea of "affliction" or "distress." The apostle Paul speaks of his tribulations for the saints at Ephesus and urges them not to lose heart on this account because such pressure would result in their "glory" (Eph. 3:13; see also 2 Cor. 7:4; 1 Thess. 3:4). To illustrate these "pressures," Jesus listed what a believer ought to expect, especially as we approach the end of the age. He selects hatred, persecution, excommunication, and death (John 15:18–20; 16:2). But with pressures, there are the divine compensations: exceeding joy (2 Cor. 7:4), comfort (1 Thess. 3:4–7), and glory (Eph. 3:13). So again, we see the vitality that issues from the suffering of tribulation.

The Vitality of Suffering through Ministration

Blessed be the God and Father of our Lord Jesus
Christ, the Father of mercies and God of all comfort,

who comforts us in all our tribulation, that we may be
able to comfort those who are in any trouble, with the
comfort with which we ourselves are comforted by
God. For as the sufferings of Christ abound in us, so
our consolation also abounds through Christ. Now if
we are afflicted, it is for your consolation and salvation, which is effective for enduring the same sufferings that we also suffer. Or if we are comforted, it is
for your consolation and salvation. And our hope for
you is steadfast, because we know that as you are partakers of the sufferings, so also you will partake of the
consolation. (2 Cor. 1:3–7)

Paul spells out the vitality of ministration in these words that we
so often quote in times of trouble. "[God] who comforts us in all
our tribulation, that we may be able to comfort those who are in
any trouble" (2 Cor. 1:4). Here I could "take off" with examples
which could fill the rest of this book and more, but I will restrict
myself to just a few.

Don Marston

The Reverend Don Marston is a seminary-trained
pastor/preacher who distinguished himself in a local church
ministry in Memphis for a number of years. All was going
well until a troublesome condition made him see the doctor.

Before my fateful day in July 1999, I knew no one at The
Memphis Cancer Center. Then Dr. Kirby Smith himself introduced me to the team of nurses. One afternoon during a
chemotherapy treatment I caught up with the Rev. Don
Marston, the Director of Patient Support. I had seen him
around and observed how caring and cheerful he was with the
patients, and I was deeply impressed. He told me later that he
knew who I was, but did not want to impose himself upon
me! However, it did not take me long to connect and converse
with him. It was during one of these "fellowship sessions"
when he responded to an urgent call to lead a dying woman to
saving faith in Christ. He told me that he had seen more con-
versions since he accepted the call to be the Director of
Patient Support than all the rest of his pastoral ministry put
together! Here is his testimony—in his own words:

In August of 1986, my wife and I were asked to
consider becoming foster parents through the Tennessee Baptist Children's Home. We understood there
was an urgent need to find homes for newborn babies.
Everyone we consulted tried to discourage us, saying
the timing was not right. We had already been richly
blessed with two preschool children. For reasons we
could not understand, we felt compelled to help with

this ministry. The Lord sent baby Stephen into our lives. Within one week, we had to find another home for Stephen.

God's purpose in my life had little to do with foster care and everything to do with getting a stubborn, thirty-one year old pastor to see a doctor. Never mind the fact that there had been unexplained weight loss, night-sweating, knots under my arm, and pronounced fatigue. In my view, these minor nuisances would go away with aspirin, time, and prayer. I was numb with disbelief to receive a diagnosis of non-Hodgkin's lymphoma in Stage IV! This form of leukemia had metastasized into my bone marrow. Dr. Kirby Smith of The Memphis Cancer Center was highly recommended to me for treatment. Although he was calm, confident, competent, kind, and quite hopeful, I perceived this diagnosis as a death sentence. Fear drained a lot of my joy. It wasn't so much a fear of dying, but of *suffering*.

The next nine months included two different protocols of chemotherapy, several hospital stays, becoming bald, lots of nausea, and losing sixty-five pounds. The nurses said most of that was to be expected. What was happening to me emotionally and spiritually caught me by surprise. The biblical texts were very familiar and I had even preached a series of sermons on handling adversity. It would be nice to say that I became a model of faith and courage, but it would not be true. Anger raised its ugly head. It took about six months to admit that much of my anger was directed at God. For some time, I wallowed in self-pity. Were it not for the patience and prayers of many, I would not have survived.

In June of 1987, a battery of tests revealed no sign of cancer. Dr. Smith then "harvested" my healthy bone marrow. If the lymphoma were to recur, we would have the option of a bone marrow transplant without having to find a donor. In September of 1989, those same tests disclosed that the cancer had returned and the bone marrow transplant became a reality. This hospital stay lasted six weeks, most of which was spent in isolation.

All aspects of transplant were much more traumatic than my previous experience. In one week, I was administered seven "total body" radiation treatments and high-dose chemotherapy. The side effects were extremely difficult to handle. My emotions went out of control, and the tears would not stop. Was I losing my mind? Depression and loneliness overwhelmed me. Where was God? Had I been forsaken? Could I truly be saved and feel what I feel? It was a very humbling experience. It occurred to me that it might be best to resign the pastorate if I lived through this ordeal. How could God ever use someone spiritually bankrupt like me? I prayed that God would take my life.

God in His infinite grace began little by little to transform my perception of this "horrible" experience. The turning began with a couple of minister friends who loved me enough to let me work through all my confusion and heartache. Their love and acceptance helped me to understand that God still loved me. It dawned on me that none of this would be wasted if I were just willing to let the Lord bring meaning to it. God planted in my heart a strong desire to come alongside others who had been jolted by this thing called cancer. For about three years, much of my pastoral ministry gravitated toward this kind of crisis ministry. It occurred to me that if there were some way to provide for my family, this could easily become a full-time ministry. In the summer of 1992, Dr. Smith and

The Memphis Cancer Center enabled me to fulfill what has become my life's calling. He created a position on staff just for me. For lack of a better name, we called it Director of Patient Support. We agreed that it would be Christ-centered, non-threatening, free of charge, and open to the community.

For almost eight years, it has been my privilege to be a small part of this special place called The Memphis Cancer Center. If there is any effectiveness to my ministry here it is in sharing openly the struggles I experienced, along with the comfort, hope, and love found in Jesus Christ. Since my arrival on staff, the center has expanded to support services through The Memphis Cancer Foundation. It is a joy to be a part of a place that provides such a full range of medical, emotional, and spiritual support. There was a time when I thought cancer was the worst thing that could have happened. God has used it to open a door to a unique ministry opportunity.

Bessie Olford

Bessie Santmire Olford is the name of my mother who is now in glory. She was born of Christian parents in Blasdell, New York, and came to Christ as her Savior and Lord at an early age. In the city of Buffalo, she later served her internship under a saintly lady known as "Sister Abigail," who wrote the booklet *Little Is Much When God Is in It.* The Bessie in that booklet is the young lady who became my mother! In 1914 Bessie went to Toronto Bible College and then on to London, England, for further medical training. With a deep sense of call to be a missionary to Africa, she left with other missionary "rookies" for Angola, where she met Frederick Ernest Samuel Olford—and two years later married him! After a distinguished missionary career and becoming a mother of three sons (Stephen, Paul, and John), we left as a family in 1935 from Lobito Bay, Angola via Lisbon, Portugal to Southampton, England. The voyage took forty-four days on a Portuguese banana boat! Throughout my mother's missionary career, she was known as a "servant-sufferer."

It was not long after the start of this long voyage that my mother found a man on a blanket at the stern of the ship—left to die. The plan was to push him overboard to his death when the order was given. The crew member had a skin problem that had erupted in boils and blains. My mother went to the captain and virtually claimed the sick man as her charge. She knew the danger of infection, but she was also a trained and experience nurse. So after prayer with the family, she committed herself to the task as a "ministry" to this dying man.

Every day she treated his sores and fed him with nourishing food, while teaching him the gospel. Upon arrival at the port in Lisbon, the crew member was not only cured but also radically converted to Christ! I can still visualize that grateful man embracing my mother and shouting for everyone to hear, "My mother, my savior, my friend."

Significantly enough, my mother had a similar skin disorder before she left Angola! She went through incredible suffering with courage and confidence in God. Little did she know that within a few months she would be "fleshing out" Paul's words, "If we are afflicted, it is for your consolation and salvation, which is effective for enduring the same sufferings which we also suffer" (2 Cor. 1:6).

Amy Carmichael

Amy Carmichael was an Irish missionary who spent fifty-three years in South India without a furlough. She founded the Dohnavur Fellowship, a refuge for children in mortal danger. For a great part of her life, she was bed-ridden with an incapacitating affliction, but she never let up in serving others by her prayers, writings, and personal counseling. The Spirit of God, to whom she was totally committed, has wafted the fragrance of her life across the Christian world. Her life and ministry are best reflected in this challenging poem:

Hast thou no scar?
No hidden scar on foot, or side, or hand?
I hear thee sung as mighty in the land,
I hear them hail thy bright, ascendant star,
Hast thou no scar?

Hast thou no wound?
Yet I was wounded by the archers, spent,
Leaned Me against a tree to die; and rent
By ravening beasts that compassed Me, I swooned:
Hast thou no wound?

No wound? No scar?
Yet, as the Master shall the servant be,
And pierced are the feet that follow Me;
But thine are whole: can he have followed far
Who has no wound nor scar?

—Amy Carmichael

Rejoice in the Life of God

"God is not the God of the dead, but of the living" (Matt. 22:32).

These weighty words were addressed to a religious sect known as the Sadducees. They did not believe in the resurrection, angels, or miracles. Their main issue, however, was the resurrection. So Jesus countered with God's great affirmation, "I am . . . the God of Abraham, the God of Isaac, and the God of Jacob" (Ex. 3:6, 15). Notice that His claim is not stated in the past tense; He does not say, "I *was* the God of Abraham!" Then come the words of our text, "God is not the God of the dead, but of the living." Our God is a great God; He transforms the "sword of suffering" into a life of vitality.

The Vitality of a Living Faith—illustrated by Abraham. "I am . . . the God of Abraham." Of Abraham it could be written:

"Faith was accounted to [him] for righteousness" (Rom. 4:9), and he became . . .

> the father of all those who believe. . . . And not
> being weak in faith, he did not consider his own body,
> already dead (since he was about a hundred years old),
> and the deadness of Sarah's womb. He did not waver
> at the promise of God through unbelief, but was
> strengthened in faith, giving glory to God, and being
> fully convinced that what He had promised He was
> also able to perform. (Rom. 4:11, 19–21)

The above verses, of course, refer to Isaac's birth.

God has recorded Abraham's faith in Scripture not to immortalize him, but to give us a model to follow. We follow Abraham's example when we believe that the God Who raised Jesus from the dead can raise us now to new life in Christ, and resurrect us one day at His coming. Our God is the God of the impossible. What vitality this gives us even in a time of suffering!

> ✴ **The Vitality of a Living Hope**—illustrated by Isaac. God
> said to Abraham, "Sarah your wife shall bear you a son, and
> you shall call his name Isaac; I will establish My covenant
> with him for an everlasting covenant, and with his descend-
> ants after him" (Gen. 17:19). When God promised a son to

Abraham, the patriarch laughed in disbelief since he was a hundred years old and his wife, Sarah, was past childbearing age. However, in spite of his initial doubt, Abraham believed God; Isaac was born, and it was then God's turn to laugh (Gen. 17:7 and 12:3). But the point to note here is that **all** the promises of God to Abraham concerning his descendants were wrapped up in his only son, Isaac (Gen. 22:17). He alone was the *"living hope."* This was not confirmed, however, until the test of Mt. Moriah (read carefully Gen. 22:1–19). God put His servant through a time of incredible suffering by telling him to sacrifice his son on Mt. Moriah. The writer to the Hebrews tells us that "by faith Abraham, when he was tested, offered up Isaac, . . . his only begotten son, . . . concluding that God was able to raise him up, even from the dead" (Heb. 11:17–19)! We know the rest of the story—God provided a substitute "ram" (Gen. 22:13). Therefore, the "living hope" was reaffirmed through suffering.

✻ **The Vitality of a Living Love**—illustrated by Jacob. "Jacob I have loved; But Esau I have hated" (Mal. 1:2, 3). This startling reference to Jacob is found amidst a legion of other references throughout the Old and New Testaments. The mention of Jacob here is both "startling" and significant. A quote from Dr. John MacArthur's study Bible is appropriate here: "The context speaks of love as 'choosing for intimate fellowship' and hate as 'not choosing for intimate fellowship' in the realm of redemption."[2] While God is addressing the descendants of Jacob and Esau, there is also the personal application. God loved Jacob in spite of his reckless and riotous life. The Bible affirms that "whom the LORD loves He chastens" (Heb. 12:6). Jacob proved this when God cornered him, crushed him, and crowned him one night at a place called Peniel (read the story in Gen. 32:24–32). The "sword of suffering" found and left its mark in Jacob's life, and he was never the same again. All this happened because God loved Jacob.

If you have been following closely, you will have noticed Paul's trilogy of "faith, hope, love" (1 Cor. 13:13). Dr. Griffith Thomas used to call it "the sum of Christian doctrine and duty." By *faith* God generates vitality in our Christian life; by *hope* God motivates vitality in our Christian life; and by *love* God radiates vitality in our Christian life—for God is not the God of the dead; God is the God of the living—even through suffering.

REJOICE IN THE LIFE OF GOD!

---

2. *The MacArthur Study Bible: New King James Version* (Nashville: Word Publishing, 1997), 136.

part two

the theology of suffering

"To this you were called, because Christ also suffered for us, leaving us an example, that you should follow His steps" (1 Pet. 2:21).

We now turn from the biographical to the theological, and this is by design. It is out of the fires of suffering that our souls cry out: Why? Why? Why? Is there a purpose behind all this? What is God doing?

This problem of suffering in all ages has engaged the greatest minds and the simplest minds. According to *Baker's Dictionary of Theology,* "the dilemma of Epicurus is still with us: if God wishes to prevent evil but cannot, then He is impotent; if He could, but will not, He is malevolent; if He has both the power and the will, whence then is evil?"[1] Questions like this would make us crazy if we did not have the recourse of the Word of God. The philosophical

---

1. *The Elements of Pain and Conflict in Human Life,* by W. R. Sorley and others, p. 48. Vol. XII:1 (Quoted in *Baker's Dictionary of Theology,* 505).

arguments concerning suffering are no more than speculations—however attractive they may be. It is significant that our Lord presented no formula relative to the why and what of suffering. Instead, He presented a way of victory in the face of suffering. What is more, He demonstrated how to live triumphantly in the midst of suffering.

Ultimately, the problem of suffering cannot be divorced from the wider and deeper problem of sin. Moreover, we know that the problem of sin can only be resolved in the cross of Christ. So the central message of the Bible from cover to cover is the reconciling grace of God in Jesus Christ. It reverberates along every rim of the universe. The triumph of this reconciliation brings the realization that "all things work together for good" (Rom. 8:28). From *Baker's Dictionary of Theology,* I quote another profound statement: "In the Christian message we find the unveiling of a suffering God. The cross is the Christian apologetic, the sublime and majestic vision"[2] of "Him who endured the cross despising the shame" (Heb. 12:2). Only in that Cross is the ultimate solution to suffering, sorrow, and separation.

> *"Ultimately, the problem of suffering cannot be divorced from the wider and deeper problem of sin."*

---

2. *Baker's Dictionary of Theology,* 505–506.

In the meantime, we are called by grace to follow Christ's *example* in suffering. We are to "trace out" in our lives His *walk* to the cross in order to understand His *work* on the cross. The walk and the work must never be confused. What Jesus accomplished at Calvary is unique and final. In that death of deaths, **all** the demands of a holy God were met through Christ's complete payment for sin. It is on this basis alone that God can declare believing sinners righteous and accept them into His family without compromise on His part.

To help us understand the need and nature of the death of Christ, I am devoting a full chapter to the subject. Instead of dealing with it topically, I have elected to present an exposition of one of the crucial passages in the New Testament. To prepare your mind and heart, I invite you to read the first eleven verses of 1 Corinthians.

CHAPTER SIX

The Suffering of the Savior

"Christ died for our sins according to the Scriptures, and . . . He was buried, and . . . He rose again the third day according to the Scriptures" (1 Cor. 15:3, 4).

The suffering of the Savior culminates in "the death of the cross" (Phil. 2:8). So the death of Christ is the pivotal fact of time. It cleaves human history in two, and is the converging point between two eternities. It is both universal and eternal in its issues. It is the touchstone of all God's dealings in this day, and will be the basis of His dealings with judgment in a day to come. Four salient truths must be noted from the verses you have read.

The Death of Christ Was Voluntary

"Christ died" (1 Cor. 15:3). Though we read that He was murdered, slain, crucified and killed, yet, in the last analysis, "Christ died"; that is to say, His death was voluntary.

It Was Voluntary as to the Motive

With the cross before Him, Christ could say, "Behold, I have come . . . to do Your will" (Heb. 10:7); "The Son of Man did not come to be served, but to serve, and to give His life a ransom for many" (Matt. 20:28); "for this purpose I came to this hour" (John 12:27). This latter statement is well paraphrased by Bishop Alford: "I came to this hour for this very purpose."[1] The cross never took the Lord Jesus by surprise. Throughout His life and ministry, it was ever before Him.

It Was Voluntary as to the Method

"Christ died" (1 Cor. 15:3). The Lord Jesus escaped death from being thrown over the precipice at Nazareth (see Luke 4:29); He escaped death by stoning many times (John 8:59; 10:31); and throughout His earthly life He knew the method of His death and told His disciples, "The chief priests and . . . the scribes . . . will condemn . . . and deliver [Me] to the Gentiles to mock and to scourge and to crucify. And the third day [I] will rise again" (Matt. 20:18, 19). Jesus had impressed the fact of His impending death upon His apostles, but the mode of His death had not been specifically mentioned. Intimations of such a death had been given by implication when He chal-

---

1. Alfred Henry, revised by E. F. Harrison. 4 vols. *The Greek Testament* (Chicago: Moody Press, 1958), 829.

lenged His followers to take up the cross and follow Him (Luke 9:23), and when He spoke of being "lifted up" like the serpent in the wilderness (John 3:14). But in this statement, (Matt. 20:19), the Master was clear and concise: the Son of Man would be *crucified.* He knew the method of His death.

It Was Voluntary as to the Moment

"Christ died" (1 Cor. 15:3). When the moment of death came He "[bowed] His head, He gave up His spirit" (John 19:30). What is indicated in those words, "bowing his head," is not the helpless dropping of the head after death, but the deliberate voluntary act of putting His head into a position of rest before dismissing His Spirit. The same verb is used in the statement in Matthew 8:20 in which He declared, "The Son of Man has nowhere to lay His head." So our Lord reversed the natural order by positioning His head, crying "with a loud voice" (Matt. 27:50), "It is finished!" (John 19:30). Thus, we see that this voluntary character of the death of Christ lifts the event right out of the realm of ordinary deaths—and even extraordinary deaths—into the place of uniqueness, infinite wonder, and redemptive significance. His death was voluntary.

The Death of Christ Was Vicarious

"For our sins" (1 Cor. 15:3). Here are words which reveal that Christ did not merely die as a martyr, but as the Bearer away of sin—"the just for the unjust, that He might bring us to God" (1 Pet. 3:18). A vicarious death means a representative death, and this verse tells us what was represented in that death:

God's Holiness Was Represented

"Christ died" (1 Cor. 15:3). Christ died to represent God's holy love and holy justice. For in that death Christ, in one crowning act, satisfied the holy claims of love and the holy claims of justice. All the righteous demands of a sin-hating and man-loving God were met. So Paul exclaims, "Christ Jesus, whom God set forth . . . to demonstrate His righteousness" (Rom. 3:24, 25). Well did the hymnist E. C. Clephane write:

> *O safe and happy shelter!*
> *O refuge tried and sweet!*
> *O trysting-place where heaven's love*
> *And heaven's justice meet!*

Sin's Heinousness Was Represented

"Christ died for our sins" (1 Cor. 15:3). Christ died to expose, bear, and judge forever man's heinous sins—"who Himself bore our sins in His own body on the tree" (1 Pet. 2:24).

If you want to see your polluted thought-life represented, look at the blood that trickled from His thorn-crowned brow. If you want to see your sins of action represented, fix your eyes upon His bleeding, nail-pierced hands. If you want to see your shameful life of waywardness represented, behold the gory spikes that held His precious feet. If you want to see the utter corruption and desperate wickedness of your heart represented, watch the crimson flow that issued from His blessed side—and then cry:

> *O wonder of all wonders,*
> *That through Thy death for me,*
> *My open sins, my secret sins,*
> *Can all forgiven be!*
> *O make me understand it,*
> *Help me to take it in,*
> *What it meant to Thee, the Holy One,*
> *To bear away my sin.*
>
> —Katherine A. M. Kelly

Man's Helplessness Was Represented

"Christ died for our sins" (1 Cor. 15:3). Christ died to reveal man's utter helplessness as a sinner, and thereby throw him entirely upon God's grace and mercy for salvation. He demonstrated this helplessness of man by self-imposed physical weakness. We read that "He was crucified in weakness" (2 Cor. 13:4). This means that even though He finally died in a conscious and strong act of triumph, sacred love compelled His willing obedience unto death in order that He might save us. Thus Paul's word is true of us all: "When we were still without strength, in due time Christ died for the ungodly" (Rom. 5:6).

THE SWORD OF SUFFERING

Guilty, vile and helpless we;

Spotless Lamb of God was He;

"Full atonement" can it be?

Hallelujah! what a Saviour!

—Philip P. Bliss

The Death of Christ Was Verified

"According to the Scriptures" (1 Cor. 15:3). The death of Christ was not just an untimely end. His death was rather the fulfillment of the Scriptures, according to "the determined purpose and foreknowledge of God" (Acts 2:23). Paul refers here, of course, to the Old Testament Scriptures. These are divided into the Law, the Psalms, and the Prophets. Paul says that Christ's death was in accordance with each of these scriptural divisions:

The Law

"Christ died . . . according to the Scriptures" (1 Cor. 15:3). The Law demanded Christ's death. M. R. DeHaan in his book, *The Chemistry of the Blood* had this to say concerning God's Law:

Long, long before the perfect Lamb of God Himself came, the Lord was preparing the world for Him by the multitudinous types in the Old Testament. Without blood, there could be no atonement, and until the blood was presented, the Holy Law of God demanded justice and death upon the sinner. That is why, when God gave the two tables of the Law to Moses upon Mount Sinai, . . . He also gave to Moses, in the same Mount, the pattern of the tabernacle which was indeed built on blood. . . . God knew when He gave the Law that [Israel would] not keep it perfectly and must die and so in mercy He gave the tabernacle and the altar and the blood so that a sinning people condemned by the Law might have life through the sheltering blood.[2]

"It is the blood that makes atonement for the soul" (Lev. 17:11). These words should be translated, "for the blood makes atonement by means of the soul," i.e., by means of the life that it contains. It is because the blood is the conveyor of the animal's life, and represents that life, that it serves to cover or make

> "It is the blood that makes atonement for the soul" (Leviticus 17:11).

atonement for the soul of the offerer of the sacrifice, who presents it instead of his own life. What a prophetic picture this is of our Sinbearer and Savior who offered Himself for us!

---

2. M. R. DeHaan, *The Chemistry of the Blood* (Grand Rapids: Zondervan, 1983), 15.

The Psalms

"Christ died . . . according to the Scriptures" (1 Cor. 15:3). The Psalms depicted Christ's death, and particularly Psalm 22, which has always been inseparably associated with the crucifixion of our Lord Jesus Christ. In fact, no passage in the whole of the Old Testament illustrates the accuracy of the Suffering Servant like this psalm. This is surely amazing when we remember that it was penned hundreds of years before the birth of Christ, when crucifixion was a Roman, not a Jewish, form of execution. This proof of biblical inerrancy is irresistible! Jesus quoted the words of this psalm when he prayed on the cross, "My God, My God, why have You forsaken Me?" (Ps. 22:1; Matt. 27:46).

The Prophets

"Christ died . . . according to the Scriptures" (1 Cor. 15:3). The Prophets declared Christ's death.

Dr. William Barclay reminds us that "the word prophet means both a **fore**-teller and a **forth**-teller. They were men who *fore*told the future; but even more they were men who *forth*told the will of God. They were men who lived close to God and who . . . went everywhere pointing men to God [emphasis added]."[3]

---

3. William Barclay, *The Acts of the Apostles* (Philadelphia: Westminster Press, 1953), 96.

The prophet Isaiah wrote: "He was wounded for our transgressions, He was bruised for our iniquities; The chastisement for our peace was upon Him, And by His stripes we are healed" (Is. 53:5). No passage in Old Testament literature more vividly and comprehensively sets forth the substitutionary and penal character of our Lord's death and subsequent triumphal resurrection like this one does.

> "He was wounded for our transgressions, He was bruised for our iniquities. . . . And by His stripes we are healed."
>
> —Isaiah 53:5

According to Francis Dixon, "twenty-five distinct prophecies recorded in the Old Testament were fulfilled within a few hours [of Christ's death], and they were fulfilled literally. How this confirms our faith in the Word of God and our trust in the purposes of God!"[4]

The Death of Christ Was Victorious

"He rose again" (1 Cor. 15:4). The virtue and value of this death are vindicated and demonstrated in Christ's victorious resurrection. His death was victorious in that, having died to put away sin, He rose as Victor over death. As the hymn goes:

---

4. Francis Dixon, *"The Place Called Calvary"* (n.d.).

Death cannot keep his prey—Jesus my Savior!

He tore the bars away—Jesus my Lord!

Up from the grave He arose,

With a mighty triumph o'er His foes;

He arose a Victor from the dark domain,

And He lives forever with His saints to reign.

He arose! He arose! Hallelujah! Christ arose!

—Robert Lowry

Observe that He rose as Victor over:

The Power of Death

"He rose again the third day" (1 Cor. 15:4). The Bible states that "through death He [destroyed] him who had the power of death, that is, the devil" (Heb. 2:14); and again: "The Son of God was manifested, that He might destroy the works of the devil" (1 John 3:8). Like David of old, who slew Goliath with the giant's own sword, so Christ on the cross defeated the devil with His own weapon of death.

The Sting of Death

"He rose again" (1 Cor. 15:4). The apostle reminds us that "the sting of death is sin" (1 Cor. 15:56). On the cross our Lord extracted the very pain of death by taking the sting into Himself, by tasting death for every man (see Heb. 2:9). Therefore, we can say, "O Death, where is your sting? O Hades, where is your victory?" (1 Cor. 15:55). The battle has been fought and the victory gained by the Crucified One.

Ponder the illustration of a young girl who fearfully fled from a wasp that flew nearby.

"Mother!" Mother! A wasp! A wasp!" cried the little girl as she ran in from the garden.

"Come here," called the mother, "and I'll protect you." Holding her daughter to her bosom, the mother said, "It's all right now, the wasp won't sting anymore."

"Why?" asked the girl inquisitively.

"Because I have taken the sting instead," explained the mother, pointing to her quickly swelling arm.

Yes, Jesus took the sting in Himself by tasting death for every man (Heb. 2:9).

The Fear of Death

"He rose again" (1 Cor. 15:4). At the cross our Lord triumphed over the fear of eternal doom, for whether men like to admit it or not, "it is appointed for men to die once, but after this the judgment" (Heb. 9:27). In that mysterious work of the cross and in His victorious resurrection, the Savior delivered those "who through fear of death were all their lifetime subject to bondage" (Heb. 2:15).

Here, then, is the very heart of our gospel—the voluntary, vicarious, verified, and victorious death of Christ. This is the Christian gospel—"Jesus Christ and Him crucified" (1 Cor. 2:2). You and I have to respond to this message. We cannot be neutral. We must accept or reject this Christ of Calvary, the Suffering Savior.

> "We cannot be neutral. We must either accept or reject this Christ of Calvary, the 'Suffering Savior.'"

Two remarkable pictures by Margaret Lindsey Williams were exhibited at the Royal Academy in the United Kingdom in 1917–18. The first, "The Devil's Daughter," shows a ballet dancer turning away from the symbol of the cross, which represents eternal life through the death of Christ. She is a young lady who trips through life like a gay butterfly. In her arms she holds Death—a hideous skull with its empty eye sockets and grinning teeth.

In the companion picture, "The Triumph," the ballet dancer is prostrate at the feet of One who is just visible in the background. Behind her are the soft lights, the stage, and the carefree symbols of her past life. The girl has dropped the ugly head of Death and now caresses the feet of the One who stands before her. A tear falls from the dancer's face. The answer is not hard to find. Above the dancer's head, held by two nail-pierced hands, is a crown of life. The One she worships is the Man of Calvary. Her life has been yielded to Him.

Captured by the triumph of this picture you can almost hear the girl singing the words of the hymn, "Calvary," by N. Shaxson:

> *Out there amongst the hills My Savior died;*
> *Pierced by those cruel nails, was crucified.*
> *Lord Jesus, Thou hast done all this for me;*
> *Henceforward I would live only for Thee.*

No one can truly surrender to the Christ of Calvary without being willing to "suffer for His sake" (Phil. 1:29). When Saul of Tarsus was gloriously converted on the Damascus road, he proceeded to the city where Ananias, God's messenger instructed him. Mark carefully the words Ananias was given by God to convey to Saul. The Lord said to Ananias, "He [Saul] is a chosen vessel of Mine to bear My name before Gentiles, kings, and the children of Israel. For I will show him how many things he must *suffer for My name's sake*" (Acts 9:15, 16; italics mine).

Later, Paul could write in one of his last epistles, "For to you it has been granted on behalf of Christ, not only to believe in Him, but also to suffer for His sake" (Phil. 1:29). This is truly an amazing verse, and is packed with profound meaning. Paul "marries" the concepts of believing and suffering. He also elevates suffering to a "gracious gift" bestowed by God. However, the deeper implication of the words "for His sake" will startle anyone reading the chapter for the first time. The language can mean "in the place of" or "instead of."

Paul interprets what he means when he defines suffering as "fill[ing] up . . . what is lacking in the afflictions of Christ, for the sake of His body, which is the church" (Col. 1:24). This verse does not imply that Christian suffering serves as a completion of Christ's atonement. The atoning work that Christ accomplished on the Cross is sufficient and complete. Colossians 1:24 refers rather to the fact that Christian suffering is a daily outworking of Christ's suffering. As Dr. Gerald F. Hawthorne puts it, Christians have been chosen to be "Christ's replacement on earth in order to suffer in His place in His absence."[5] Are you and I willing to take joyfully upon ourselves the burden of Christ's suffering in history what still remains to be borne?

I share these precious and profound truths in order to show what the cross should mean and *do* in our lives. In the chapter to follow, this line of thinking will be expanded; but here and now I want us all to agree with George MacDonald when he affirmed that "the Son of God suffered unto . . . death, not that men might not suffer, but that their sufferings might be like His."[6]

---

5. *Word Biblical Commentary: Philippians,* vol. 43 (Waco, Texas: Word Books, 1983), 61.

6. C. S. Lewis, *The Problem of Pain* (New York: Macmillan Co., 1965), flyleaf.

Respond to the Love of God

"For the love of Christ constrains us, because we judge thus: that if One died for all, then all died; and He died for all, that those who live should live no longer for themselves, but for Him who died for them and rose again" (2 Cor. 5:14, 15).

The suffering of the Savior evoked deep emotions in the experience of the great apostle Paul. The phrase, "the love of Christ," means *His* love for *us*, as demonstrated in His sacrificial death. That is why we can exclaim with John the Apostle, "We love Him because He first loved us" (1 John 4:19). When we consider the reasons why Christ died, we cannot help but *love* Him. Think about this love for a moment:

In love He died that we might die. "We judge thus: that if One died for all, then all died" (2 Cor. 5:14). This truth is explained in detail in Romans 6. In essence, the truth is simply this: When Christ died, we died *in* Him and *with* Him. So the old life has no hold on us today. All the demands of a holy God against sin were borne by our matchless Savior on the cross, and we are free! "[We] have been crucified with Christ" (Gal. 2:20). Thank Jesus for this!

In love He died that we might live. "He died for all, that those who live should live no longer for themselves, but for Him who died for them and rose again" (2 Cor. 5:15). This is the positive aspect of our oneness with Christ. We can now "reckon [ourselves] dead indeed to sin, but *alive* to God in Christ Jesus our Lord" (Rom. 6:11). With Paul we can testify: "It is no longer I who live, but Christ lives in me . . . by faith in the Son of God, who *loved* me and gave Himself for me" (Gal. 2:20). This is the liberating love of Christ living in us. The life we cannot live He lives in us as we trust Him moment by moment in restful faith. Just pause and thank Jesus again for this liberating love. Because of this liberating love:

* **We Can Live THROUGH Christ**—"God . . . sent His only begotten Son into the world, that we might live *through* Him" (1 John 4:9).

* **We Can Live FOR Christ**—"He died for all, that those who live should live no longer for themselves, but *for* Him" (2 Cor. 5:15).

* **We Can Live WITH Christ**—"Our Lord Jesus Christ . . . died for us, that whether we wake or sleep, we should live together *with* Him" (1 Thess. 5:10).

Those precious prepositions ("through," "for," and "with") should make us "dance for joy"!

RESPOND TO THE LOVE OF GOD!

CHAPTER SEVEN

The Suffering of the Saint

"Beloved, do not think it strange concerning the fiery trial which is to try you, as though some strange thing happened to you; but rejoice to the extent that you partake of Christ's sufferings, that when His glory is revealed, you may also be glad with exceeding joy" (1 Pet. 4:12, 13).

Suffering is perhaps the greatest problem we have to face in this life. It is a subject of complexity to explain and of perplexity to experience. To penetrate its mysteries is to be faced with such issues as the suffering of saints, the suffering of sinners, the suffering of innocents, and the suffering of animals.

In this chapter, however, we will focus on the **suffering of the saint**. Second only to the suffering of the Savior, we have more revealed to us on this aspect of suffering than on any of the other categories I have listed.

However, before delving into our main subject, one important thing must be said about the lost—those outside of Christ. C. S. Lewis, in his masterly book, *The Problem of Pain,* likens pain or suffering to a megaphone that God uses to warn men and women to forsake their evil ways. He writes: "It may lead [a man] to final and unrepented rebellion. But it gives the only opportunity the bad man can have for amendment. It removes the veil; it plants the flag of truth within the fortress of a rebel soul."[1] The "flag of truth" is nothing less than *repentance* toward God, by turning away from our sins; *acceptance* of Christ as Savior, who died for our sins and rose to be Lord of our lives; and *dependence* on the Holy Spirit for "life and godliness" (2 Pet. 1:3).

But now we turn to our theme for this chapter—The Suffering of the Saints. One of the first lessons we learn from the Word of God concerns:

The Promise of Suffering

"Beloved, do not think it strange concerning the fiery trial which is to try you, as though some strange thing happened to you; but rejoice to the extent that you partake of Christ's sufferings" (1 Pet. 4:12, 13). Peter uses those words "do not think it strange" to prepare the hearts of his readers to expect suffering. It is both promised

---

1. C. S. Lewis, *The Problem of Pain* (New York: Macmillan Co., 1965) 83.

and normal! Indeed, Jesus taught that suffering would happen in the home, in the church, and in the world.

Suffering in the Home

"A man's enemies will be those of his own household" (Matt. 10:36). Read the context in Matthew 10:32–39. If we confess Christ with our lives as well as with our lips, we can expect conflict and suffering even in our homes (Matt. 10:32–35). A stand for Christ can "set a man against his father, a daughter against her mother, and a daughter-in-law against her mother-in-law" (Matt. 10:35). It is a fact of life that believers in a non-Christian home often suffer more hostility and cruelty in the home than in the world. The pain of this suffering is intense simply because the "enemies will be those of [their] own household" (Matt. 10:36).

> *"It is a fact of life that believers in a non-Christian home often suffer more hostility and cruelty in the home than in the world."*

Suffering in the World

Blessed are those who are persecuted for righteousness' sake, For theirs is the kingdom of heaven. Blessed are you when they revile and persecute you, and say all kinds of evil against you falsely for My sake. Rejoice and be exceedingly glad, for great is your reward in heaven, for so they persecuted the prophets who were before you. (Matt. 5:10–12)

In this eighth beatitude we have a description of the true Christian's impact upon the world and the reaction of a Christ-rejecting world to the Christian. If there is no persecution of any kind, then the Christian might well question the integrity of his devotion to Christ. Studying our Lord's prediction of suffering for the believer, we notice three clear aspects of attack by a satanically-controlled world-system:

There is **spiritual opposition.** "Blessed are you when they revile . . . you" (Matt. 5:11). To "revile" means to look down upon another as vile and low. Being reviled involves being despised and rejected of men. It is important to observe that this hatred against the Christian is essentially spiritual. Spiritual opposition does not come to a Christian simply because he or she lives a noble life or performs noble deeds (even though this should be true of a Christian); but rather because he/she is indwelt by Jesus Christ, and the spirit of hatred is the spirit of antichrist.

Secondly, there is **personal accusation.** "Blessed are you when they . . . say all kinds of evil against you falsely for My sake" (Matt. 5:11). Hatred of the genuine Christian may take the form of slander. In early church history, there were certain slanderous reports spread abroad concerning Christian belief and behavior, which ultimately led to suffering and death.

Thirdly, there is **physical persecution.** "Blessed are you when they . . . persecute you" (Matt. 5:11). Although the word "persecution" has a much wider application, it originally conveyed the idea of bodily injury. In order of sequence, this is how hatred expresses itself: first, opposition; then accusation; and finally, persecution. This has been true of saints down through the centuries. Think of Abel who was murdered by his brother Cain. Think of David who was hounded and hunted by King Saul. Think of Daniel who was hated by his jealous enemies. Think of Stephen who was stoned to death. Think of James who was slain with the sword. Think of Paul who was persecuted beyond measure. Think of the apostles, most of whom died the martyr's death.

> *Ponder the words of Jesus: "If the world hates you, you know that it hated Me before it hated you."*
> —John 15:18

Pause for a moment and read slowly Hebrews 11:35–40.

Lest we should be taken by surprise by such hatred and consequent suffering and tribulation, we must recall the words of Jesus when He said, "If the world hates you, you know that it hated Me before it hated you" (John 15:18).

This brings us to:

The Purpose of Suffering

"Rejoice to the extent that you partake of Christ's sufferings, that when His glory is revealed, you may also be glad with exceeding joy" (1 Pet. 4:13). If this were the only verse in the Bible about the purpose of suffering it would be sufficient, but we have more to follow!

What Peter is saying (see context in 1 Pet. 4:12–19) is that the Christian attitude to suffering should be positive and purposeful. To be a partaker of the sufferings of Christ is a cause for rejoicing. The verb "rejoice" is in the present tense demanding not a single isolated response, but a continuous attitude and activity. It means that, as Christians, we should welcome the privilege to share in the outworking of God's age-long purpose, according to which the Lord Jesus enters His glory, through suffering (Luke 24:26; 1 Pet. 1:10,11). In the meantime, there are three aspects of suffering which help us to see the essential purpose of suffering:

Suffering Chastens Us for God's Purpose

". . . do not despise the chastening of the LORD, Nor be discouraged when you are rebuked by Him; For whom the LORD loves He chastens" (Heb. 12:5, 6; see also vv. 7–11). The writer to the Hebrews links suffering and sonship (see also Proverbs 3:11, 12). Moreover, the word "discipline" combines the thoughts of chastening and education. It points to the sufferings that teach us what God has in mind for each of His children. The writer has just highlighted "striving against sin" (v. 4), and suggests that in this struggle, God's hand of chastening is involved—*because He loves us* (v. 6). And to what purpose is this chastening and suffering? The answer is crystal clear: "that we may be partakers of His holiness," and that we may "[yield] the peaceable fruit of righteousness" (vv. 10, 11). So suffering *chastens* us for God's purpose.

Suffering Cleanses Us for God's Purpose

"He will sit as a refiner and a purifier of silver; He will purify the sons of Levi" (Mal. 3:3). Chastening and cleansing are similar concepts, but each has its own identity. Chastening projects the notion of punishment, whereas cleansing implies purification. I have selected this Old Testament verse because it vividly depicts the cleansing process to make us purified and qualified "priests" unto God. In light of the imminence of Christ's Second Coming, we are to see to it that we are cleansed and ready (1 John 3:3). John the Apostle makes "no bones" about it! "Little children," he says, "abide in Him, that when He appears, we may have confidence and not be ashamed before Him at His coming" (1 John 2:28). According to Malachi 3:2, there are two purifying agents to make us clean: *fire* for metals, and *soap* for clothing. Just as these agents remove impurities, so God "employs" the fire of burning (the Holy Spirit; Is. 4:4) and the water of cleansing (the Holy Word; Eph. 5:26; Titus 3:5) to purify us for earthly service now and heavenly service in the age to come. Burning off the dross and washing off the filth involve suffering, but this is part of God's eternal purpose in making us "a royal priesthood, a holy nation, His own special people, that [we] may proclaim the praises of Him who called [us] out of darkness into His marvelous light" (1 Pet. 2:9).

Suffering Captures Us for God's Purpose

As Christians, our ambition should be to "know Him [Christ] and the power of His resurrection, and the fellowship of His sufferings, being conformed to His death, if, by any means, [we] may attain to the resurrection from the dead" (Phil. 3:10, 11). Here is where we reach the level of "water in which [we] must swim" (Ezek. 47:5). We can no longer wade; we either swim or sink. We are now captured and carried by the current of the river. Paul had done everything when he dictated this beautiful letter to the saints at Phillipi. He had evangelized major cities, planted churches, written theology, languished in prison, suffered every form of punishment and persecution and was at the end of his life and ministry. What was left to be done or said? Listen again to his words from a different translation, "I want to know Christ and the power of his resurrection and *the fellowship of sharing in his sufferings*" (Phil. 3:10, NIV). Paul had entered a dimension of suffering which completely captured him. He no longer suffered *for* Christ—which is persecution. From this point onward in Paul's ministry, he suffered *with* Christ—which is passion.

A Passion for a Groping World. "I tell the truth in Christ, I am not lying, my conscience also bearing me witness in the Holy Spirit, that I have great sorrow and continual grief in my heart. For I could wish that I myself were accursed from Christ for my brethren, my countrymen according to the flesh" (Rom. 9:1–3). Paul understood what the prophet Isaiah meant when he described the outworking of God's redemptive plan in Christ in those prophetic words, "He shall see the labor [travail] of His soul, and be satisfied" (Is. 53:11). Paul shared this passion, and other saints have shared it likewise. Amy Carmichael shared it when she wrote:

> *O for a passionate passion for souls,*
> *O for a pity that yearns!*
> *O for the love that loves unto death,*
> *O for the fire that burns.*

A Passion for a Growing Church. It is Paul again writing, this time to the Galatians, "My little children, for whom I labor [travail] in birth again until Christ is formed in you"

(Gal. 4:19). And similarly to the saints in Colosse, "I now rejoice in my sufferings for you, and fill up in my flesh what is lacking in the afflictions of Christ, for the sake of His body, which is the church" (Col. 1:24). Do you, do I, have a passion for the growth of the Church? Do we travail in prayer and ministry until Christ is formed in the lives of the saints? Perhaps the reason why so-called converts never seem to grow up is that we know nothing of the suffering of Christ in us and through us to make this happen.

A Passion for a Groaning Creation. "For we know," writes Paul, "that the whole creation groans and labors [travails] with birth pangs together until now. Not only that, but we also who have the firstfruits of the Spirit, even we ourselves groan within ourselves, eagerly waiting for the adoption, the redemption of our body" (Rom. 8:22, 23). "We know," states Paul. However, how many **really** know what this poor old creation is suffering today? Let us remember that every expression of cruelty, every decaying carcass of poor earth's creatures, speaks of the bondage of corruption which man's sin has caused. Jesus will never be satisfied until His purposes in creation and redemption are realized. In prophetic language Isaiah expresses it this way: "He shall see the travail of His soul and be satisfied" (Is. 53:11; see also Rom. 8:18–25). Do you and I share this suffering to bring to birth the fruits of His redemptive work?

The question now arises as to how we can ever share this suffering with Christ. The answer according to the apostle is "being conformed to His death" (Phil. 3:10). Paul *lived* for Christ because he *died* to self (Romans 6 explains this); he took up his cross daily and followed Jesus (Luke 9:23). In short—for you and me—it is fleshing out Galatians 2:20, "I have been crucified with Christ; it is no longer I who live, but Christ lives in me; and the life which I now live in the flesh I live by faith in the Son of God, who loved me and gave Himself for me." This happens to be my life's verse!

> *How can we share suffering with Christ? We can do this only when we live "being conformed to His death."*
>
> —Philippians 3:10

Mrs. A. A. Whiddington expresses Galatians 2:20 beautifully:

> *Oh, to be saved from myself, dear Lord,*
> *Oh, to be lost in Thee;*
> *Oh, that it may be no more I,*
> *But Christ {who} lives in me.*

One last aspect of suffering must detain us. It is:

The Profit of Suffering

"Rejoice to the extent that you partake of Christ's sufferings, that when His glory is revealed, you may also be glad with exceeding joy" (1 Pet. 4:13). Can you catch the exuberance and excitement of Peter? He looks on to that day when Christ's destined glory is universally manifested and acknowledged. In that day, every tongue will declare that Jesus is Lord. So to suffer now with rejoicing prepares us to rejoice then with inexpressible exaltation.

So what is the profit of suffering? The answer is twofold:

The Joy of Sharing Heaven with a Rewarding Lord

"Blessed are you when they revile and persecute you, and say all kinds of evil against you falsely for My sake. Rejoice and be exceedingly glad, for great is your *reward* in heaven, for so they persecuted the prophets who were before you" (Matt. 5:11). Life here upon earth is not the end, but merely a means to an end. This is a probation period; the *reward* is fullness of life in that eternal beyond.

In addition to this, the Scriptures are replete with teaching on rewards that await the believer at the Judgment Seat of Christ. There is, for instance, the reward of the Savior's *commendation*. "Well done, good and faithful servant. . . . Enter into the joy of your lord" (Matt. 25:21).

Furthermore, there is the reward of the Savior's *crowns*. Six of them, at least, are mentioned in the New Testament. These crowns represent authority and responsibility in the eternal kingdom of Christ and His Father. They also will forever demonstrate the measure of one's faithfulness while here on earth. No wonder John, in his second epistle, warns, "Look to yourselves, that we do not lose those things we worked for, but that we may receive a full reward" (2 John 1:8).

The Joy of Sharing Heaven with a Reigning Lord

"If we endure [suffer], we shall also reign with Him" (2 Tim. 2:12). "If indeed we suffer with Him, that we may also be glorified together" (Rom. 8:17). Sharing in the suffering of Christ may be looked on as simply the cost of discipleship, and that is true; but such suffering has a brighter aspect. It is the prelude to reigning with Christ in the coming glory. This takes us back to our original text: "Rejoice to the extent that you partake of Christ's sufferings, that when His glory is revealed, *you may also be glad with exceeding joy*" (1 Pet. 4:13; italics mine). The prospect of such rapturous joy should be a compelling reason for continuing joy, even while still in the midst of suffering (see Rom. 5:2, 3; 12:12).

For those who forget such truths as these, Paul has to ask: "Do you not know that the saints [that is you and I] will judge the world? . . . Do you not know that we shall judge angels?" (1 Cor. 6:2, 3). The context of these two verses has to do with Christians going to secular courts against one another. What concerned Paul was that the Corinthians were failing to exercise their divine prerogatives to settle such problems within the community of the church. With that as a background he asks, "Do you not know that the saints [those who are holy—God's people] will judge the world. . . . judge angels?" He is writing in light of that day when we will reign with Christ! (Rom. 8:17).

So the profit of suffering is sharing heaven with the rewarding Lord—yes, and a reigning Lord—in a day that is coming. May the Lord hasten that day!

Until we hear "the shout" (see 1 Thess. 4:16), let us remember that "our light affliction, which is but for a moment, is working for us a far more exceeding and eternal weight of glory, while we do not look at the things which are seen, but at the things which are not seen. For the things which are seen are temporary, but the things which are not seen are eternal" (2 Cor. 4:17, 18). "Therefore we do not lose heart" (2 Cor. 4:16).

St. Ignatius of Loyola crafted an appropriate prayer (known as the "Prayer for Generosity") with which we can appropriately conclude this chapter . . .

Teach us, good Lord, to serve Thee as Thou deservest:
To give and not to count the cost;
To fight and not to heed the wounds;
To toil and not to seek for rest;
To labor and not to ask for any reward
Save that of knowing that we do Thy will.

STEPHEN F. OLFORD

Rely on the Purpose of God

"And we know that all things work together for good to those who love God, to those who are the called according to His purpose. For whom He foreknew, He also predestined to be conformed to the image of His Son" (Rom. 8:28, 29).

In our text Paul tells us that we never need be concerned in times of suffering and trial because *God is working out all things for our good according to His purpose.* That purpose is always twofold: it is for our *good* and for His *glory.* Ultimately, God's redemptive purpose is to conform us to the image of His Son (v. 29). We can rely on this purpose for at least three reasons:

✶ **The Certainty of God's Word to Us**—"We know that all things work together for good" (Rom. 8:28). The verb *know* means more than intellectual comprehension: it implies *personal experience* based upon God's word of promise.

✷ **The Alchemy of God's Work in Us**—"We know that all things *work together*" (Rom. 8:28). "Work together" is a phrase from the world of chemistry. Like a pharmacist, our wonderful God knows the measure and the mixture of ingredients that are best for each one of us.

✷ **The Sovereignty of God's Will for Us**—"And we know that all things work together for good to those who are the called according to His purpose. For whom He foreknew, He also predestined to be conformed to the image of His Son, that He might be the firstborn among many brethren. Moreover whom He predestined, these He also called; whom He called, these He also justified; and whom He justified, these He also glorified" (Rom. 8:28–30). In sovereign grace we have been called, justified, and glorified. The Apostle uses the past tenses to stress our eternal security in Christ. I can think of no better words to sum up the truth of God's purpose for our lives—you and me—than the words of the great hymn, "How Firm a Foundation":

> *Fear not, I am with thee, O be not dismayed,*
> *For I am thy God, I will still give thee aid;*
> *I'll strengthen thee, help thee, and cause thee to stand,*
> *Upheld by My gracious, omnipotent hand.*
>
> *When through fiery trials thy pathway shall lie,*
> *My grace all-sufficient shall be thy supply;*
> *The flame shall not hurt thee; I only design*
> *Thy dross to consume, and thy gold to refine.*

RELY ON THE PURPOSE OF GOD!

CHAPTER EIGHT

The Suffering of the Servant

"My grace is sufficient for you, for My strength is made perfect in weakness" (2 Cor. 12:9; see vv. 7–10).

Suffering, as we have seen already, is a fact of life. To attempt to dispute or dismiss this fact is utterly foolish, for suffering is all around us. We see it in the home, etched in the face of an ailing loved one. We hear it from the streets in the agonizing groans of some victim mugged by thugs. We catch it in the news from war-torn areas of the world.

Suffering has been the lot of all people, including the greatest men of God who ever lived. Of these we could mention such biblical characters as Job, Jeremiah, Paul, and, of course, our Lord Himself.

As we consider the subject of the suffering of the servant, we think particularly of Paul the Apostle. Throughout His life He experienced what he termed "a thorn in the flesh" (2 Cor. 12:7). Martin Luther maintained that this affliction represented the opposition and persecution which Paul had to face. John Calvin's view was that the "thorn" symbolized spiritual temptation. Then there are others who argue from the Scriptures (Gal. 4:15; 6:11) that, in all probability, the thorn in the flesh was a form of eye trouble, stemming from the blinding glory that Paul experienced on the Damascus road (see Acts 9:9). Still others speculate that Paul's problem could have been any malady ranging from malaria, epilepsy, insomnia, or depression. Obviously, there is no way we can know for sure what form of suffering is represented by Paul's "thorn." Such uncertainty may be providential, because Paul's experience helps us to understand our own sufferings and how we can rise above them.

There Is a Mystery in Suffering

Paul says, "Lest I should be exalted above measure by the abundance of the revelations, a thorn in the flesh was given to me, a messenger of Satan to buffet me" (2 Cor. 12:7). We cannot read these words in the context of the Bible without coming to the conclusion that the problem of suffering is enveloped in mystery. There are, however, two facts that we need to bear in mind as we attempt to unravel the mystery:

The Mystery in Suffering Is Linked with the Morality of God's Creatures

Paul says, "A thorn in the flesh was given to me" (2 Cor. 12:7). Strange as it may seem, his suffering is traced to the permissive action of an all-wise God. When God created angels, and later man, He did not produce robots; on the contrary, He brought into being personalities capable of moral decisions. To have done anything less would have failed to express His own character. In view of this, man is free to choose to enthrone God or to dethrone Him. The Bible teaches that Satan chose to dethrone God. Adam did likewise in the Garden of Eden and, through this moral sin of rebellion, suffering inevitably followed. Suffering, therefore, has become part of human life; something to be accepted until that day when God will remove all sin from this world and usher in "new heavens and a new earth in which righteousness dwells" (2 Pet. 3:13).

Herbert Lockyer wrote a book entitled *A Dark Thread the Weaver Needs*. It is a book on human suffering and how we wrestle with it. Dr. Lockyer named his book after a poem written by Grant Colfax Tullar. The poem reads like this:

My life is but a weaving, between my Lord and me,
I cannot choose the colors, He worketh steadily.
Oftimes He weaveth sorrow, and I, in foolish pride,
Forget He sees the upper, and I the underside.

Not till the loom is silent and the shuttles cease to fly,

Shall God unroll the canvas and explain the reason why.

The dark threads are as needful in the Weaver's skillful hand,

As the threads of gold and silver in the pattern He has planned.

The Mystery in Suffering Is Linked with the Mortality of God's Creatures

"A thorn in the flesh was given to me" (2 Cor. 12:7). In this statement, Paul spells out his own mortality. When Adam sinned he affected himself and the whole of the human race, for the Bible says, "Through one man sin entered the world, and death through sin" (Rom. 5:12). Because man is mortal, he is subject to all manner of infirmities. It is true that temperament, environment, bereavement, or ailment may accentuate the various forms of suffering; but the fact remains that suffering is a problem to be reckoned with. Sometimes tribulation may come in the form of spiritual suffering; other times as mental suffering; but most frequently in the form of physical suffering.

Georgi Vins spent most of fifteen years in prison—three at hard labor. He was completing the fifth year of his sentence to be followed by five years of exile in Siberia. Suddenly he was given a suit, a shirt, and a tie and was told that he had been stripped of Soviet citizenship. Within forty-eight hours, he found himself in the United States. Authorities arrested his sixty-eight-year-old mother for aiding Christians and sentenced her to three years in prison. Georgi was only seven years old the last time he saw his father, who died in prison. When Bill Moyers interviewed Georgi, he said, "Your father died in prison; your mother was arrested. You've spent much of your life in prison. You once wrote, 'Our life has not been given for empty dreaming.' What has it all meant? What do you think our lives signify?" His reply: "I do not regret the years I have spent, even the years of suffering. This has been the purpose of my living."

> "I do not regret the years I have spent, even the years of suffering. This has been the purpose of my living."
>
> —Georgi Vins

As we have observed already in these chapters, God promised Paul a life of suffering from the very outset of his conversion. God's message to Saul of Tarsus was clear and convincing: "I will show him how many things he must suffer for My name's sake" (Acts 9:16). What happened to Paul has happened to God's servants throughout the centuries, and will continue to happen in your lifetime. In a very real sense, we are God's "suffering servants." Never in the history of the Church, have so many of God's servants sealed their testimonies in blood as in this past century. In the last fifty years alone, more Christians were martyred than at any other time since the Day of Pentecost.

There Is Agony in Suffering

"A thorn in the flesh was given to me" (2 Cor. 12:7). When Paul speaks of his "thorn," he uses a word that does not appear on the surface. The term "thorn" means a "stake," and it seems as if Paul used this word to convey the intensity of suffering which he experienced.

The Extent of This Suffering

"A thorn in the flesh was given to me, a messenger of Satan to buffet me" (2 Cor. 12:7). In the sovereignty of God, this "messenger of Satan" was allowed to assault and attack the Apostle at every corner of the road. The word "buffet" means "to strike with the blow of the fist," and so conveys the idea of shame and humiliation in addition to suffering. As we study the life of the Apostle, it seems that he was ever up against the devil. In Cyprus, he had to face Elymas the sorcerer, whom Paul described as the "son of the devil" (Acts 13:10). In Thessalonica, the devil prevented him from visiting that church (see 1 Thess. 2:18). In Ephesus, he tells us that he "fought with beasts" (1 Cor. 15:32); and later, writing to that same church, he declares, "We do not wrestle against flesh and blood, but against principalities, against powers, against the rulers of the darkness of this age, against spiritual hosts of wickedness in the heavenly places" (Eph. 6:12).

The Effect of This Suffering

"Concerning this thing I pleaded with the Lord three times that it might depart from me. And He said to me, 'My grace is sufficient for you'" (2 Cor. 12:8, 9). As long as we are in this world, we shall suffer pain. We have already established the principle that God allows pain, but the devil also employs the "thorn." What determines triumph or defeat, however, is finally decided by the effect of the pain. If the pain leads to resistance and resentment, then the consequence is one of depression and despair. On the other hand, if the pain leads to prayerfulness and patience, then the result is one of maturity and victory. Like his Master before him, Paul prayed three times for deliverance from "the thorn in the flesh." He asked for faith and persistence, but the "thorn" was never removed. Instead, the answer from heaven was, "My grace is sufficient for you, for My strength is made perfect in weakness" (2 Cor. 12:9).

There Is Victory in Suffering

"Most gladly I will rather boast in my infirmities, that the power of Christ may rest upon me. Therefore I take pleasure in infirmities, in reproaches, in needs, in persecutions, in distresses, for Christ's sake. For when I am weak, then I am strong" (2 Cor. 12:9–10). Paul here reaches the climax of his subject. Suffering certainly means agony, but it can also mean victory. As long as we walk the pilgrim pathway, we shall know joy and experience sorrow; but the evidence of having learned the lessons in the school of obedience is that we emerge "more than conquerors through Him who loved us" (Rom. 8:37). This victory in Christ is determined by the exercise of our faith.

There Is a Test of Faith

> Therefore I take pleasure in infirmities, in re-
> proaches, in needs, in persecutions, in distresses, for
> Christ's sake. For when I am weak, then I am strong.
> (2 Cor. 12:10)

Imagine a man saying, "*I take pleasure* in infirmities, in reproaches, in necessities, in persecutions, in distresses, for
Christ's sake!"

The story is told of a man who was asked to visit a lady
dying of an incurable and painful disease. He took with him a
little book of cheer for those in trouble. "Thank you very
much," she said, "but I know this book." "Have you read it already?" asked the visitor. With a smile on her face, the woman
replied, "I wrote it." Faith in our Lord who suffered even unto
death gives us the victory in times of affliction and depression.
In the place of weakness, He ministers His grace and strength.

There Is Rest in Faith

"Most gladly I will rather boast in my infirmities, that the
power of Christ may rest upon me," or more literally, that "the
dynamism of Christ might overshadow me" (2 Cor. 12:9). Paul
knew that, as long as he gloried in his Lord in times of infirmities, a "tabernacle" of power would overshadow him. His
weakness was the secret of his strength. On the other hand, if

he gloried in anything other than Christ, that tent of power would be removed.

Think of it this way. We know that electric power comes from the turbulent pressure of accumulated masses of water backed up by a dam and forced through turbines, which generate electricity. Steam power comes by fire, which heats the water until it expands and creates pressure in a cylinder. Gasoline combustion power is the explosion of a volatile liquid in a chamber called a cylinder, thus setting in motion a piston head and crankshaft.

I use the descriptions of electric, steam, and gasoline combustion power to illustrate "the strength of suffering principle." The principle is thus: as we rest by faith in Christ to employ what He pleases to discipline and develop our lives, we find that the very pressures He uses are transmitted into power. The moment we resist, the power is removed; as we rest in faith, the power remains. Instead of being a problem, suffering can become a redemptive power.

George Matheson, noted poet and man of God, lost his sight as a youth and spent thirty years in darkness. The third stanza of one of his widely-known hymns reads:

> *O Joy that seekest me through pain,*
> *I cannot close my heart to Thee;*

I trace the rainbow through the rain,
And feel the promise is not vain
That morn shall tearless be.

George Matheson had learned to live with his darkness. More than that, he had learned the benefits of his handicap. His victory is seen in the words he once wrote:

My God, I have never thanked thee for my thorn. I have thanked thee one thousand times for my roses, but never once for my thorn. I have been looking forward to a world where I shall get compensation for my cross, but never thought of my cross as a present glory. Teach me the glory of my cross. Teach me the value of my thorn. Show me that I have climbed to Thee by the path of pain. Show me that my tears have been my rainbow.[1]

History is replete with illustrations of servants of God who have been used in the world because they have suffered. The supreme example is our Lord Jesus Christ, who, through His suffering on the cross, provided us with forgiveness, freedom, and fruitfulness. Let us then kneel now at the foot of that cross and bow to the Holy Spirit, who enabled Him to suffer even unto death, to produce in us the same fruits of victory. There is mystery in suffering; yes, and agony, but, thank God, there is also victory!

---

1. B. J. Woods, *Understandable Suffering* (Grand Rapids: Baker Book House, 1974).

Receive the Grace of God

"He gives more grace. Therefore He says: 'God resists the proud, but gives grace to the humble'" (James 4:6; read also vv. 1–9).

The verses that precede and follow this text are important, if we would understand the need for "more grace." You and I received "grace" from God when we were saved. The Bible reminds us that "by grace [we] have been saved through faith, and that not of [ourselves]; it is the gift of God" (Eph. 2:8). But now James writes about "more grace." Why more grace? The answer is: to resist and conquer the world (v. 4), the flesh (vv. 1, 2), and the devil (v. 7)— our threefold enemy!

The attack of the enemy is never more cruel and constant than when we are suffering or sorrowing as God's servants. The world taunts us, the flesh flaunts us, and the devil daunts us! In and of ourselves we can do nothing. We need "more grace"—overflowing grace and overcoming grace; but there are conditions:

✴ **We Must Be Helpless**—"God resists the proud" (James 4:6). As long as we exalt ourselves, as sufficient of ourselves, we are headed for defeat and disaster. Counting on the grace of God is evidence of acknowledged helplessness and dependence. Paul needed grace and received grace and proved it sufficient for him.

✴ **We Must Be Humble**—"God . . . gives grace to the humble" (James 4:6). It is one thing to be helpless, but quite another matter to be humble. Many times I have been helpless, but not humble enough to ask for "more grace." Grace is "**G**od's **R**iches **A**t **C**hrist's **E**xpense." Think about that.

✴ **We Must Be Holy**—"Draw near to God and He will draw near to you. Cleanse your hands, you sinners; and purify your hearts, you double-minded" (James 4:8). These are tough words, but they are true words. God will not pour His grace into unclean vessels. So often we want God's grace while we hold on to our sins. But God says, "Cleanse your hands, you sinners." In the language of Augustus M. Toplady (1740–1778), we need to pray right now:

> *Nothing in my hand I bring,*
> *Simply to Thy cross I cling;*
> *Naked, come to Thee for dress,*
> *Helpless, look to Thee for GRACE;*
> *Foul, I to the fountain fly,*
> *Wash me, Savior, or I die!*

RECEIVE THE GRACE OF GOD!

part three

the psychology of suffering

A PSYCHOLOGICAL PERSPECTIVE

BY JONATHAN M. OLFORD, PSY.D.

Some of the marvelous lessons suffering offers to us have been shared, for there are many different types of suffering in the world. Some of the pain we experience may be reduced to sin done to others and sin done to us. Either way, at its root, one can easily realize that suffering came into the world as a partner with sin. And there is inevitably a strong linkage between living in a fallen world and the experience of suffering and pain. As a psychologist, I primarily engage with people in their suffering. Often their suffering may be so painful, that the only role I can initially play is to partner with them in their pain. Such partnership comes by offering the peace of tranquility through sharing that is inextricably linked to a prayer uttered in an attitude of dependency brought about by suffering. However, the essence of one's suffering is often reflected in a different manner than that of pain as we typically think of it.

Today's suffering takes many forms. There are obviously those who suffer physical pain and illness. The suffering of the individual recovering from the bruises, cuts, and lacerations of a car accident, or a child recovering from a bad case of the flu alerts us to a level of pain and discomfort that most of us have had to endure, some even on a daily basis. Our newspapers and magazines, journals, radio and TV news, and our gossipmongers inform us daily of the latest painful reminders of our human frailty. Our minds are constantly barraged with the latest atrocities on our freeways, in our schools, and atrocities perpetually endured by those in war, or those experiencing persecution and injustice a world away in countries like Sudan and China.

These reminders draw to our awareness the significance of physical pain and distress, hunger and loss, as well as the absence of easy answers when the pain becomes so great that we literally are unsure as to whether or not we will ever make it through to the other side. Just as pain and suffering vary in many forms, so do the ways we choose to cope with it or, in some cases, choose not to cope with it.

Apparent Mental and Emotional Suffering

Many forms of familial and individual circumstances cause us pain. The pain and suffering often associated with broken relationships carry significant weight in our culture. With numbers indicating that still more than fifty percent of couples are terminating their marriages, we remain a people and a culture in denial over the pain that this relatively simplistic act of divorce is most likely to kindle in the lives of both marriage partners and the children caught in the crossfire. This pain affects the mind, and it can manifest itself in various ways. For instance, suffering minds may evidence their intense internal conflict and confusion in severe mental and emotional distress, in physical pain and symptoms, or in alienation and interpersonal detachment. Symptoms we commonly see and identify with may include the commonality of depression, overwhelming panic and anxiety, or some form of addictive behavior. Insomnia, rumination, "acting out" and other impulsive behaviors may also serve as telltale signs of the suffering mind.

Suppressed Suffering (Denial)

Perhaps the most-difficult-to-understand category of suffering within the Christian arena lies in the area of suppressed feelings and emotions. Whether or not the psychological suffering is caused by emotional, physical, or spiritual precipitants, many of us tend to harbor feelings of sorrow, depression, sadness, and despair because the feelings are so overwhelming that we simply choose not to face them. Of course, ignoring pain is not always possible, for happiness is not simply a choice. Therefore, we often dodge the pain because we are both afraid of what we might feel, as well as what those feelings might do to us.

There are also those times, as well as circumstances, that cause us to feel that we are wrong when we examine our emotions. Part of us may say, "Forget feelings, just perform," or, "Christians should not acknowledge or walk by feelings." This approach to the management of our emotions often finds its root in having been raised in an environment where feelings were not appreciated or shared. To exemplify this, imagine for a moment a little boy on his roller blades falling on the sidewalk. He scrapes his knee and howls with pain just as his father arrives home from work. Well-meaning Dad comes over to his crying son and states, "That doesn't look so bad; what'cha crying for?" The little boy knows that his leg hurts, sees the blood, but also acknowledges that the person in whom he has implicit trust has just defined his feelings of pain out of existence. The boy has been told, "It's not that bad."

It is often because of repeated experiences, as the example just mentioned, that we develop the habit of suppressing emotions—or of disowning them. In so doing, we establish a coping style that, in fact, may last a lifetime. At times, our so-called composure or "self-control" may be mistaken for deep faith. Whether or not the message is intentional, when we suppress feelings caused by suffering, we communicate that sorrow, sadness, pain, and anguish are simply not compatible with a genuine deep and lasting faith.

Suffering Caused by Tragedy

Shootings like the one at Columbine High School or an unanticipated diagnosis of cancer are representative of human tragedy and pain. The fear, the worry, and the impact on loved ones all symbolize enormous obstacles to overcome. Yet we often forget that the greatest catastrophe occurred so many years ago when Adam, by a single act of disobedience, submerged all of mankind in a sea of misery and sorrow.

It has become so easy in this day and age to forget the reality of suffering. Most of us have the great fortune of living in a country and in a time that, by comparison, is so blessed with freedoms, economic prosperity, and comfort-making technology. With so much wealth and leisure, we often lose sight of reality and perhaps are numbed or seduced into believing a lie. The harsh reality is that our world, while containing much that is beautiful, is lived out under a curse. This world has been distorted and disfigured by the ravages of the Fall, which God is patiently and relentlessly laboring to overcome.

Christians are not spared the effects of the Fall. It is true that we do not grieve as those who have no hope (2 Thess. 4:13). It is also true that the deaths and suffering of the wicked or the righteous do not frustrate God's loving purposes. Therefore, it is important that we remind ourselves of the profound comfort only attainable in the knowledge that God is both sovereign and good.

The notion that one can control the events, demands, or stress associated with pain and suffering is simply a fantasy! We are stuck with our environments, for better and often *for worse!* Nevertheless, what we can learn to do, aided by our sovereign Lord, is to manage our response to our environment. Just as it is misguided to think that we can manage our circumstances, it is misguided to think that we are reduced to merely *reacting* to them.

In response to this reality, a jeweler and artisan friend of mine drew attention to a wonderful image. Referencing the biblical allusion to the concept of "living stones" (1 Pet. 2:5), my friend asked me if I could think of a "living stone." Having to give the question some thought I acknowledged that I could not. My friend then took the opportunity to educate me on the nature of the oyster. The oyster takes in a piece of grit. This speck of sand becomes a constant irritant to the life and reality of the oyster. The oyster combats its suffering by surrounding the speck of sand daily with a substance called *nacre.* As the layers of nacre build on one another and as the oyster lives with and manages its suffering, a beautiful pearl is formed. The slow process of the developing pearl serves to define the appeal this rough, ugly, and seemingly insignificant oyster has to each of us. Within this brown, insignificant-looking shell is a pearl, a *"living stone"* that represents the suffering life of the oyster itself.

The psalmist writes, "The Lord is near to those who have a broken heart, And saves such that have a contrite spirit" (Ps. 34:18). The word for "broken" in this passage in the original Hebrew language is *shabar,* which means "crushed." The Hebrew word for "contrite" is *dakka,* which means "reduced to dust," or, more literally, "powdered."

So the secret of the power emanating from loss and suffering occurs when we learn to handle suffering well. Loss humbles us. Pain reminds us that we are not God and that we do, in fact, need Him. Throughout the Psalms, we see the intimate struggle of those driven to God by the desperate circumstances of their lives. There were times, as I read the Psalms as a kid, that I wondered why God allowed David to express himself the way he did. In the Psalms, it seems that David often complains; he whines; he shouts and expresses the extremes of grief, anger, fear, and other negative human emotions. However, David also expresses praise, supreme humbleness and an incredible sense of peace in the realization of the depth of his relationship with his Creator. It should be clear that it is the former portrait of David, in those isolative, negative, anguish-filled moments, that serve to drive us to the Comforter.

We live in a world defined by universal suffering. This is one of psychology's most fundamental positions; that people do have problems and suffer. Even good, Bible-believing, Spirit-filled people have problems. However, recognizing that there are those willing to act in Christlike love, to sit and be with us and to engage in relationship with us even when we have been crushed to *powder,* enables us to create that *living stone* that becomes the *pearl of great price* (see Matt. 13:46).

POSTSCRIPT

A pastor friend of mine, Larry Burd, of Calvary Baptist Church, Bethlehem, Pennsylvania, sent me the following testimony when I was facing disease—and possibly despair. Thank God I never succumbed to despair. His testimony was a precious comfort to me. Here it is:

{All Scripture quotations in this testimony are from the King James Version.}

At about 7:30 p.m. on Tuesday, December 12, 1995, the telephone rang. It was my doctor, who said, "We have the results from your biopsy, and we discovered that you have a malignant tumor on your prostate gland."

The word *cancer* is one of the most frightening words a person can ever hear, especially when it comes to you personally from your doctor. It shocked me when I heard it. A cold numbness gripped my heart, and many thoughts raced through my mind. What will happen to me as a result of having cancer? Will I live or die? What about my wife and four children? What about my ministry and all the dreams and goals for my life?

After putting down the telephone, I went to my bedroom to pray. I told God about my problem, and then surrendered my life to His perfect will regardless of what it might involve. I had learned to trust Him during difficult times in the past, and I resolved to trust Him with the problem of cancer as well. A deep assurance and peace calmed my fears. I knew that God was with me and would help me.

Opening my Bible, I read Psalm 112. The seventh verse says, "He shall not be afraid of evil tidings [bad news]: his heart is fixed, trusting in the LORD." Those words were incredible! I could trust God with my fears, anxieties, and all my concerns. I could trust Him with my whole life. I could trust Him to give me courage and strength to face the future. I could trust Him to heal me if it were His will, and I could trust Him to help me if it were not His will to heal me.

I chose not to ask God, "Why do I have cancer," but instead asked, "What do you want me to learn from this?"

Have you ever thought about how limited cancer really is? An unknown author wrote the following words:

POSTSCRIPT

WHAT CANCER NEED NOT DO

Cancer is so limited . . .

It need not cripple love,

It need not shatter hope,

It need not corrode faith,

It need not eat away peace,

It need not destroy confidence,

It need not kill friendship,

It need not shut out memories,

It need not silence courage.

Where do you turn in a time of crisis? Where do you turn when you need guidance, strength, courage, hope, and the ability to cope with the trials of life?

When I was 17 years old, I made the most important decision of my life. I became a Christian. God used the life story of Bobby Richardson, a professional baseball player with the New York Yankees, to speak to me about my need for a personal relationship with God through faith in Jesus Christ. Bobby Richardson said, "Jesus Christ means more to me than anything else in the world." At first, I thought he was a religious fanatic, and I wasn't interested in learning any more about his life. But the more I read, the more interested I became.

Bobby Richardson described God in such a personal way. He said, "God so loved the world, that he gave his only begotten Son, that whosoever believeth in him should not perish, but have everlasting life" (John 3:16).

I knew in my heart that I did not deserve God's love and that I had sinned before a holy and righteous God. The Bible says, "For all have sinned, and come short of the glory of God" (Rom. 3:23). But the Bible also said, "For the wages of sin is death, but the gift of God is eternal life through Jesus Christ our Lord" (Rom. 6:23).

How could I have a personal relationship with God? How could I be certain that I would have eternal life and go to heaven someday? I came to realize that I could not save myself, but that I needed a Savior. "For by grace are ye saved through faith; and that not of yourselves: it is the gift of God: not of works, lest any man should boast" (Eph. 2:8, 9).

The Bible tells us that "Christ died for our sins according to the scriptures; and that He was buried, and that He rose again the third day according to the scriptures" (1 Cor. 15:3, 4). The thought that Jesus Christ loved me enough to die for my sins penetrated my heart and mind. I wanted to be forgiven of my sins. I was

POSTSCRIPT

willing to repent and turn away from anything I thought would displease God. With all my heart I wanted to know Jesus Christ in a personal way.

One day I prayed a prayer (by faith) similar to this one:

"God, if You are really up there, and if Jesus Christ is truly Your Son, and if He died on the Cross for my sins, and if He is alive right now, then I want to know Him personally. I ask You to forgive me of all of my sins. I am sorry for my sins. By faith, I open the door of my heart and invite You to come into my life. Please change me and help me to know You are real. Thank You for giving me the gift of eternal life. In Jesus' name I pray, Amen."

That prayer changed my life eternally. I began to experience a peace and joy I had never known before. Second Corinthians 5:17 became a reality to me. "Therefore, if any man be in Christ, he is a new creature; old things are passed away; behold, all things are become new."

Are you faced with the problem of cancer or some other seemingly impossible situation in your life? The Bible says, "For with God nothing shall be impossible" (Luke 1:37). God can do what no other power can do.

POSTSCRIPT

I want to encourage you to turn to God in all of life's joys and sorrows. Talk to Him in prayer like you would talk to a close friend. Read the Bible. It's still the world's best seller. As you read, ask God to reveal Himself to you.

If you have never invited Jesus Christ to come into your life, please pray the kind of prayer I prayed, and He'll become real to you too.

The motto of my life is, "HE DIED FOR ME; I'LL LIVE FOR HIM."

The destructive forces of cancer can bring sorrowful consequences, but the disease cannot separate us from God's love. Romans 8:38, 39 says, "For I am persuaded, that neither death, nor life, nor angels, nor principalities, nor powers, nor things present, nor things to come, nor height, nor depth, nor any other creature, shall be able to separate us from the love of God, which is in Christ Jesus our Lord."

Only Jesus Christ can give you eternal life. I recommend Him to you. If you have not already done so, give your life to Him right now.

"BEHOLD, NOW IS THE ACCEPTED TIME; BEHOLD NOW IS THE DAY OF SALVATION" (2 COR. 6:2b).

"Whatever things were written before were written for our learning, that we through the patience and comfort of the Scriptures might have hope" (Rom. 15:4).

The Companionship of God

Joshua 1:5–9

No man shall be able to stand before you all the days of your life; as I was with Moses, so I will be with you. I will not leave you nor forsake you. Be strong and of good courage, for to this people you shall divide as an inheritance the land which I swore to their fathers to give them. Only be strong and very courageous, that you may observe to do according to all the law which Moses My servant commanded you; do not turn from it to the right hand or to the left, that you may prosper wherever you go. This Book of the Law shall not depart from your mouth, but you shall meditate in it day and night, that you may observe to do according to all that is written in it. For then you will make your way prosperous, and then you will have good success. Have I not commanded you? Be strong and of good courage; do not be afraid, nor be dismayed, for the LORD your God is with you wherever you go.

Psalm 23

The LORD is my shepherd;
I shall not want.
He makes me to lie down in green pastures;
He leads me beside the still waters.
He restores my soul;
He leads me in the paths of righteousness
For His name's sake.

Yea, though I walk through the valley of the shadow of death,
I will fear no evil;
For You are with me;
Your rod and Your staff, they comfort me.

You prepare a table before me in the presence of my enemies;
You anoint my head with oil;
My cup runs over.
Surely goodness and mercy shall follow me

All the days of my life;

And I will dwell in the house of the LORD

Forever.

Isaiah 43:1–3

. . . Fear not, for I have redeemed you;

I have called you by your name;

You are Mine.

When you pass through the waters, I will be with you;

And through the rivers, they shall not overflow you.

When you walk through the fire, you shall not be burned,

Nor shall the flame scorch you.

For I am the LORD your God,

The Holy One of Israel, your Savior. . . .

Matthew 28:20

Lo, I am with you always, even to the end of the age. Amen.

Hebrews 13:5, 6

He Himself has said, "I will never leave you nor forsake you." So we may boldly say: "The LORD is my helper; I will not fear. What can man do to me?"

Revelation 22:20, 21

He who testifies to these things says, "Surely I am coming quickly." Amen. Even so, come, Lord Jesus!

The grace of our Lord Jesus Christ be with you all. Amen.

The Compassion of God

Psalm 111

Praise the LORD!

I will praise the LORD with my whole heart,
In the assembly of the upright and in the congregation.

The works of the LORD are great,
Studied by all who have pleasure in them.
His work is honorable and glorious,
And His righteousness endures forever.
He has made His wonderful works to be remembered;
The LORD is gracious and full of **compassion**.
He has given food to those who fear Him;
He will ever be mindful of His covenant.
He has declared to His people the power of His works,
In giving them the heritage of the nations.

The works of His hands are verity and justice;
All His precepts are sure.
They stand fast forever and ever,
And are done in truth and uprightness.
He has sent redemption to His people;
He has commanded His covenant forever:
Holy and awesome is His name.

The fear of the LORD is the beginning of wisdom;
A good understanding have all those who do His
commandments.

His praise endures forever.

Lamentations 3:22–26

Through the LORD'S mercies we are not consumed,
Because His **compassions** fail not.
They are new every morning; Great is Your faithfulness.
"The LORD is my portion," says my soul,
"Therefore I hope in Him!"

The LORD is good to those who wait for Him,
To the soul who seeks Him.
It is good that one should hope and wait quietly
For the salvation of the LORD.

Matthew 6:25–34

Therefore I say to you, do not worry about your
life, what you will eat or what you will drink; nor
about your body, what you will put on. Is not life
more than food and the body more than clothing?
Look at the birds of the air, for they neither sow nor
reap nor gather into barns; yet your heavenly Father
feeds them. Are you not of more value than they?
Which of you by worrying can add one cubit to his
stature? So why do you worry about clothing?

Consider the lilies of the field, how they grow: they neither toil nor spin; and yet I say to you that even Solomon in all his glory was not arrayed like one of these. Now if God so clothes the grass of the field, which today is, and tomorrow is thrown into the oven, will He not much more clothe you, O you of little faith? Therefore do not worry, saying, "What shall we eat?" or "What shall we drink?" or "What shall we wear?" For after all these things the Gentiles seek. For your heavenly Father knows that you need all these things. But seek first the kingdom of God and His righteousness, and all these things shall be added to you. Therefore do not worry about tomorrow, for tomorrow will worry about its own things. Sufficient for the day is its own trouble.

1 Peter 5:5–11

Likewise you younger people, submit yourselves to your elders. Yes, all of you be submissive to one another, and be clothed with humility, for "God resists the proud, But gives grace to the humble." Therefore humble yourselves under the mighty hand of God, that He may exalt you in due time, casting all your care upon Him, for He **cares** for you. Be sober, be vigilant; because your adversary the devil walks about like a roaring lion, seeking whom he may devour.

Resist him, steadfast in the faith, knowing that the same sufferings are experienced by your brotherhood in the world. But may the God of all grace, who called us to His eternal glory by Christ Jesus, after you have suffered a while, perfect, establish, strengthen, and settle you. To Him be the glory and the dominion forever and ever. Amen.

The Comfort of God

Psalm 71

In You, O LORD, I put my trust;
Let me never be put to shame.
Deliver me in Your righteousness, and cause me to escape;
Incline Your ear to me, and save me.
Be my strong refuge,
To which I may resort continually;
You have given the commandment to save me,
For You are my rock and my fortress.

Deliver me, O my God, out of the hand of the wicked,
Out of the hand of the unrighteous and cruel man.
For You are my **hope**, O Lord GOD;
You are my trust from my youth.
By You I have been upheld from birth;
You are He who took me out of my mother's womb.
My praise shall be continually of You.

I have become as a wonder to many,

But You are my strong refuge.

Let my mouth be filled with Your praise

And with Your glory all the day.

Do not cast me off in the time of old age;

Do not forsake me when my strength fails.

For my enemies speak against me;

And those who lie in wait for my life take counsel together,

Saying, "God has forsaken him;

Pursue and take him, for there is none to deliver him."

O God, do not be far from me;

O my God, make haste to help me!

Let them be confounded and consumed

Who are adversaries of my life;

Let them be covered with reproach and dishonor

Who seek my hurt.

But I will **hope** continually,

And will praise You yet more and more.

My mouth shall tell of Your righteousness

And Your salvation all the day,

For I do not know their limits.

I will go in the strength of the Lord GOD;

I will make mention of Your righteousness, of Yours only.

O God, You have taught me from my youth;

And to this day I declare Your wondrous works.

SELECTED SCRIPTURES

Now also when I am old and grayheaded,

O God, do not forsake me,

Until I declare Your strength to this generation,

Your power to everyone who is to come.

Also Your righteousness, O God, is very high,

You who have done great things;

O God, who is like You?

You, who have shown me great and severe troubles,

Shall revive me again,

And bring me up again from the depths of the earth.

You shall increase my greatness,

And **comfort** me on every side.

Also with the lute I will praise You—

And Your faithfulness, O my God!

To You I will sing with the harp,

O Holy One of Israel.

My lips shall greatly rejoice when I sing to You,

And my soul, which You have redeemed.

My tongue also shall talk of Your righteousness all the day
long;

For they are confounded,

For they are brought to shame

Who seek my hurt.

Psalm 86:1–17

Bow down Your ear, O LORD, hear me;

For I am poor and needy.

Preserve my life, for I am holy;

You are my God;

Save Your servant who trusts in You!

Be merciful to me, O Lord,

For I cry to You all day long.

Rejoice the soul of Your servant,

For to You, O Lord, I lift up my soul.

For You, Lord, are good, and ready to forgive,

And abundant in mercy to all those who call upon You.

Give ear, O LORD, to my prayer;

And attend to the voice of my supplications.

In the day of my trouble I will call upon You,

For You will answer me.

Among the gods there is none like You, O Lord;

Nor are there any works like Your works.

All nations whom You have made

Shall come and worship before You, O Lord,

And shall glorify Your name.

For You are great, and do wondrous things;

You alone are God.

Teach me Your way, O LORD;

I will walk in Your truth;

Unite my heart to fear Your name.

I will praise You, O Lord my God, with all my heart,

And I will glorify Your name forevermore.

SELECTED SCRIPTURES

For great is Your mercy toward me,

And You have delivered my soul from the depths of Sheol.

O God, the proud have risen against me,

And a mob of violent men have sought my life,

And have not set You before them.

But You, O Lord, are a God full of compassion, and gracious,

Longsuffering and abundant in mercy and truth.

Oh, turn to me, and have mercy on me!

Give Your strength to Your servant,

And save the son of Your maidservant.

Show me a sign for good,

That those who hate me may see it and be ashamed,

Because You, LORD, have helped me and **comforted** me.

Isaiah 40:1–5

"**Comfort**, yes, **comfort** My people!"

Says your God.

"Speak **comfort** to Jerusalem, and cry out to her,

That her warfare is ended,

That her iniquity is pardoned;

For she has received from the LORD's hand

Double for all her sins."

The voice of one crying in the wilderness:

"Prepare the way of the LORD;

Make straight in the desert

A highway for our God.

Every valley shall be exalted

And every mountain and hill brought low;

The crooked places shall be made straight

And the rough places smooth;

The glory of the LORD shall be revealed,

And all flesh shall see it together;

For the mouth of the LORD has spoken."

Isaiah 49:8–13

Thus says the LORD:

"In an acceptable time I have heard You,

And in the day of salvation I have helped You;

I will preserve You and give You

As a covenant to the people,

To restore the earth,

To cause them to inherit the desolate heritages;

That You may say to the prisoners, 'Go forth,'

To those who are in darkness, 'Show yourselves.'

They shall feed along the roads,

And their pastures shall be on all desolate heights.

They shall neither hunger nor thirst,

Neither heat nor sun shall strike them;

For He who has mercy on them will lead them,

Even by the springs of water He will guide them.

I will make each of My mountains a road,

And My highways shall be elevated.

Surely these shall come from afar;

Look! Those from the north and the west,

And these from the land of Sinim."

Sing, O heavens! Be joyful, O earth!

And break out in singing, O mountains!

For the LORD has **comforted** His people,

And will have mercy on His afflicted.

Isaiah 51:1–3

"Listen to Me, you who follow after righteousness,

You who seek the LORD:

Look to the rock from which you were hewn,

And to the hole of the pit from which you were dug.

Look to Abraham your father,

And to Sarah who bore you;

For I called him alone,

And blessed him and increased him."

For the LORD will **comfort** Zion,

He will **comfort** all her waste places;

He will make her wilderness like Eden,

And her desert like the garden of the LORD;

Joy and gladness will be found in it,

Thanksgiving and the voice of melody.

Isaiah 61:1–3

"The Spirit of the Lord GOD is upon Me,

Because the LORD has anointed Me

To preach good tidings to the poor;

He has sent Me to heal the brokenhearted,

To proclaim liberty to the captives,

And the opening of the prison to those who are bound;

To proclaim the acceptable year of the LORD,

And the day of vengeance of our God;

To **comfort** all who mourn,

To **console** those who mourn in Zion,

To give them beauty for ashes,

The oil of joy for mourning,

The garment of praise for the spirit of heaviness;

That they may be called trees of righteousness,

The planting of the LORD, that He may be glorified."

2 Corinthians 1:3–7

Blessed be the God and Father of our Lord Jesus Christ, the Father of mercies and God of all **comfort**, who **comforts** us in all our tribulation, that we may be able to **comfort** those who are in any trouble, with the **comfort** with which we ourselves are **comforted** by God. For as the sufferings of Christ abound in us, so our **consolation** also abounds through Christ. Now if we are afflicted, it is for your **consolation** and salvation, which is effective for enduring the same sufferings which we also suffer. Or if we are **comforted**, it is for your **consolation** and salvation. And our **hope** for you is steadfast, because we know that as you are partakers of the sufferings, so also you will partake of the **consolation.**

2 Corinthians 4:13–18

And since we have the same spirit of faith, according to what is written, "I believed and therefore I spoke," we also believe and therefore speak, knowing that He who raised up the Lord Jesus will also raise us up with Jesus, and will present us with you. For all things are for your sakes, that grace, having spread through the many, may cause thanksgiving to abound to the glory of God. Therefore we do not lose heart. Even though our outward man is perishing, yet the inward man is being renewed day by day. For our light affliction, which is but for a moment, is working for us a far more exceeding and eternal weight of glory, while we do not look at the things which are seen, but at the things which are not seen. For the things which are seen are temporary, but the things which are not seen are eternal.

2 Thessalonians 2:16, 17

Now may our Lord Jesus Christ Himself, and our God and Father, who has loved us and given us everlasting **consolation** and good **hope** by grace, **comfort** your hearts and establish you in every good word and work.

Dr. Kirby L. Smith established The Memphis Cancer Center in 1976 and has introduced innovations that have both elevated the standards of cancer care in the community and have been emulated by other oncology practices throughout the region. The Memphis Cancer Center has satellite offices in Arkansas, Mississippi, and Tennessee.

The Memphis Cancer Center treats all cancers, including breast, lung, liver, prostate, brain, colon, pancreatic, as well as hematological diseases such as leukemia and lymphoma. Patients come to The Memphis Cancer Center from throughout the Mid-South and across the U.S. We are proud to be St. Jude's primary referral site for adult patients.

Area cancer patients no longer are forced to travel beyond the Mid-South for advanced treatment options. If a patient chooses, he/she may participate in clinical trials using the world's most promising investigational drugs. With the establishment of The Memphis Cancer Center's Research Division in 1999, clinical trials of existing and investigational drugs as well as new treatment modalities are now available in Memphis. These clinical studies enable qualified patients to have the advantage of the latest research findings before they are available to the general public. Specific studies are available for newly-diagnosed patients as well as for those for whom conventional treatments have not proven effective.

The Memphis Cancer Center always provides patients with exceptional education, spiritual resources, rehabilitation, and support services throughout every stage of their cancer journey. Additionally, the Center offers medically-based knowledge about integrative, complementary therapies.

Memphis Cancer Center Mission Statement

The Memphis Cancer Center is dedicated to the caring for patients and their families through the most advanced treatments available given in an atmosphere of love and respect.

Our commitment is to the whole person . . . to treat the body, to calm the mind, and to uplift the spirit of all.

The Memphis Cancer Foundation

Healthcare innovations that stretch well beyond the confines of traditional medical practices have been the forte of The Memphis Cancer Foundation since its creation in 1988. The Memphis Cancer

Foundation introduced complementary therapies to Memphis with such then "radical" ideas as support groups for cancer patients.

The Foundation has supported a number of innovations that have become mainstays of committed medical practices throughout the region. Much to our gratification, other area practices and foundations have successfully replicated many of our programs resulting in enhanced cancer patient care. Foundation support has enabled presentation of the first structured patient education programs about living with cancer.

The Memphis Cancer Center
1068 Cresthaven Road
Memphis, TN 38119

info@memphiscancercenter.com

P.O. Box 757800, Memphis, TN 38175-7800
Tel.: (901)757-7977 ✦ Fax: (901) 757-1372
Internet: www.Olford.org ✦ E-mail: OMI@Olford.org

OUR HISTORY

The Stephen Olford Center for Biblical Preaching was dedicated on June 4, 1988 in Memphis, Tennessee. It is the international headquarters for Olford Ministries International and houses the Institute for Biblical Preaching.

The Institute for Biblical Preaching was founded in 1980 to promote biblical preaching and practical training for pastors, evangelists, and lay leaders. After 50 years of pastoral and global ministry, Dr. Olford believes that the ultimate answer to the problems of every age is the anointed expository preaching of God's inerrant Word. It is Dr. Olford's sincere desire that such preaching be restored to contemporary pulpits around the world.

OUR STRATEGY

The purpose of the Institute for Biblical Preaching is to equip and encourage pastors and laymen in expository preaching and exemplary living so that that the church will be revived and the world will be reached with the saving Word of Christ. The program includes:

- Institutes and special events on expository preaching, pastoral leadership, essentials of evangelism, the fullness of the Holy Spirit, the reality of revival, and other related subjects.

- Workshops for pastors and laymen to preach "live" in order to have their sermons and preaching skills critiqued constructively.

- One-Day Video Institutes on Anointed Biblical Preaching hosted in churches around the country.

- Consultations on pastoral and practical matters.

- Outreach through wider preaching/teaching ministry, radio broadcasting, literature, audio/video resources, and our internet site.

90062